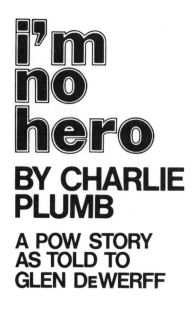

BY CHARLIE PLUMB

A POW STORY AS TOLD TO GLEN DeWERFF

Illustrated by Alta Adkins

Library of Congress Catalog Card No. 73-87637

ISBN 0-937539-38-4

Printed in the United States of America

First Printing, November, 1973

Published by:

Executive Books
206 West Allen Street
Mechanicsburg, PA 17055
800-233-2665
www.executivebooks.com

i'm no hero

To the families of those brave men
who will never return.

contents

foreword

July 1967 found Read Mecleary and me holed up in a camp we called Plantation. Read had been badly injured during his ejection, and while I was in the process of getting him on his feet, we were both trying to acclimate ourselves to life in a Communist prison.

Part of our acclimation process was to find out who was in the camp with us. Read had related to me that one of the prisoners was a Naval Academy classmate of his, to wit—one Charles Plumb. Charlie had been shot down 19 May 1967 while on a mission against a military complex nicknamed Little Detroit, just south of Hanoi.

It wasn't too many days before we heard a hoarse whisper from outside one of our boarded-up windows. "Read, can you hear me?" As quickly as he could hobble, Read got to the window and discovered through a crack in one of the boards that it was his old classmate Charlie Plumb. This, of course, was my first introduction to Charlie. Our conversation was brief, but before the guard returned, we had established a note pickup point in the toilet where we emptied our night-soil buckets. Thus was born the camp-wide communication system at the Plantation.

Charlie was at the far end of the warehouse on the other side of the camp. While he set up communications at his end, we did the same thing at ours, the goal being to link up in the middle by tap code and notes. We spent hours painstakingly putting messages together, writing on scraps of paper with the end of our toothpaste tube. Before long, Charlie's notes started to arrive, written in red ink. We could hardly believe our eyes. Red ink? How did a guy get red ink into a North Vietnamese clink? We discovered that, if his name was Plumb, and if he had the imagination of Winston Churchill and the audacity of Willie Sutton, it was no sweat. He merely stole some of the medic's mercurochrome, sharpened slivers of bamboo on the floor, and Eureka, he had ink and a pen.

How we looked forward to those notes. It would literally take us hours to decipher Charlie's double-talk. He had used this, of course, to thoroughly confuse the Vietnamese, even if they should intercept one of his messages. The initial contact over, we went to work in earnest to get everyone in camp on the line. This chore required hour after hour of waiting for just the right moment to whisper to a fellow POW his instructions about making contact. My patience wore terribly thin at times with what I considered to be snail-like progress. Charlie's notes, though, always radiated encouragement, determination, and the patience of Job.

By the first part of April 1968 we had linked up the entire camp. We felt that it was none too soon, since peace talks were in the wind. We were fairly well set up when Read, Charlie, and I moved with others from the Plantation to a different camp. I didn't see Charlie until the fall of 1970 when a group of us were moved to the country to a prison nicknamed Camp Faith. Charlie was there and we finally were able to shake hands and become better acquainted. The stay at Faith was cut short by the raid at Son Tay in November.

By Christmas we were living together in the Hanoi Hilton, the old French prison in downtown Hanoi. Soon, Charlie and I joined forces to be our room's communication team. I discovered that, in addition to his other attributes, he was extremely long on tact. While attempting to guide the seniors, who at times could be rather curt, he started what I called Charlie's Senior Officer Guidance and Training Program. He took my needle extremely well, but continued to promote his feelings about how our newly formed Fourth Allied POW Wing could best proceed. On occasion he would be admonished by someone who had rolled out on the wrong side of his mat, but his good humor, imagination, and desire to improve our organization never wilted. He displayed an almost unbelievable energy and craving for knowledge, and I found myself working with a friendly and cheerful but truly fierce competitor.

On Saturday nights, Charlie and I performed a ritual; we would sit under my mosquito net and talk into the early hours. These conversations were far-ranging, and as the months dragged on we became quite familiar with each other's philosophies. I found that my conversational partner was a good Christian, an excellent officer—matured far beyond his years; a careful thinker who, although basically conservative, could be amazingly aggressive. This aggressiveness, however, was always tempered by an acute sense of timing.

Naturally, our conversations included home, our wives, and children—born and unborn. Supplementing these wonderful memories, we both had pictures which had started coming to us in late 1970 and early 1971. I had several of the beautiful home my wife Verna had purchased in 1970. It wasn't too long before Charlie had used his keen imagination to sketch a detailed floor plan of the house. Shortly after our release he visited us and took us on a tour of our own home.

Charlie reminded me on more than one occasion of the stirring line:

> Give me some men who are stout-hearted men
> Who will fight for the rights they adore.

He is truly a stout-hearted, dedicated American— exceptionally well qualified to tell the POW story.

Jack L. Van Loan
Lieutenant Colonel
U.S. Air Force

dedication

It was a hot-coffee night at the ball park. Ardent Royals fans, bundled under their wool blankets, compared final-score predictions and gave the home team any benefit of a doubt. Then came an interruption from the loudspeaker:

"Ladies and gentlemen. Eighteen years ago, major league baseball became a part of our great city, and at that time we were honored to have President Harry S Truman throw out the first ball to introduce our new team, the Kansas City Athletics. Tonight, throwing out the first ball and dedicating this magnificent new stadium in honor of President Truman, we have another distinguished gentleman, a man who has just returned to his home after spending nearly six years as a prisoner of war in North Viet Nam. Ladies and gentlemen, please give a warm welcome to Lieutenant Commander Joseph Charles Plumb."

The massive computerized scoreboard coordinated 60,000 lights into a production resembling the finale at a fireworks display. The hubbub of 40,000 spectators echoed off the outfield wall, and the stadium itself seemed to lift a full three feet as fans spontaneously stood to applaud. I had just returned from six years of confinement, with only my enterprising imagination free to roam at will. In all that time, however, I failed to fathom such a spectacle as this.

I had been waiting in the dugout, accompanied by the owners of the Royals ball club, Muriel and Ewing Kauffman, who epitomized warmth and compassion—qualities which the North Vietnamese radio had endlessly hammered to be nonexistent in the American social elite. That those of the moneyed class were ogres or mechanical robots bent on persecuting the poor, as promised by North Vietnamese propaganda, could not have been further from the truth. The Kauffmans were congenial, down-to-earth human beings.

A bat boy offered his blue felt cap; I put it on and handed him my white naval officer cap. One of the players tossed me his glove. Suddenly I became self-conscious—wearing a baseball cap and being out of proper uniform. But, then, what better symbolic attire could represent both the military and the civilian?

Behind his catcher's paraphernalia, tobacco-chewing Jerry May lumbered up and handed me three baseballs. I quipped, "Jerry, what kind of signal are you going to give me?"

"I don't know, Commander. What do you want?"

"I have no idea, but we ought to get it straightened out. If you want a knuckle ball, I'll throw you a knuckle ball."

Jerry, still working on his tobacco, was amused but did not laugh. "You just go out there and throw anything you want."

"It may be really wild, Jerry, so be ready for anything. I haven't tossed at a plate for seven years."

That was the truth . . . but barely. Earlier that afternoon

a Royals public relations man had taken me out on the field so that I could get a feel of the ball. On the way to the mound, we were dowdily stopped by a supersensitive grounds man. "Hey, you guys, get out of here!"

I stopped the PR man. "That's OK," I said. "I wouldn't want to throw my arm away anyhow."

The grounds man thought that we were just a couple of kids who dared to enter the field and disrupt his work, and when he discovered our purpose, he was most apologetic. I left the field, still not knowing whether I could hit the strike zone.

But now it was for real. I stepped out on the field, trembling from excitement and exhaustion, and I wished that I'd had the chance to practice throwing at the plate. The cold night suddenly became colder, and the roars exceeded the roar. I was surprised at how close the mound was from the dugout, allowing even less time to prepare myself mentally. I looked down and noticed how carefully the grounds crew had prepared the field: even inconsequential clods of dirt seemed numbered.

I held the ball in my right hand and, until I reached the mound, carried the other two balls in the glove—the PR man told me that photographers wanted extra shots. I dropped the two balls and popped the remaining ball in my glove a couple of times, at the same time spotting a rosin bag at my feet. Well, I thought, why not play the role? That rosin bag's in my way anyhow. I'll kick it if I don't pick it up. So I picked it up and dusted my clammy hands. More cheers and howls erupted as the fans played the pantomime with me.

Any proximity of the pitch toward the plate would be good enough to satisfy the crowd. I put my foot on the rubber and scoped out the catcher, who was by this time going through all kinds of hand signals. The fans, still on their feet, hushed. Where in the world would this ball end up? "Dear God," I entreated, "help me put this one down the chute."

I wound up, raised my left leg, and cautiously released the ball. It was an arced slow-ball . . . right over the plate! The announcer called it a strike, and no one was more surprised than I. Supportive laughter volleyed out as I grinned at my good fortune.

Jerry trotted out, handing the ball back to me:

"Well done . . . really good!"

"Thanks, Jerry, but do you think the coach will buy it?"

"All right, Commander. We've got two more for the press."

My second ball was in the dirt. The third was high and outside. I should have quit while I was still ahead. I scampered off the field, relieved to be back in the dugout. Players were beginning to come on the field, and I handed the glove back to its owner. The bat boy and I exchanged hats, and then the PR man escorted me through garish flashbulbs to the bleachers where my dad, three uncles, and my date Kathy Melcher waited to go with me to the stadium club. I saw very little of them the rest of the night.

I was on the move again, approaching an area kept under close surveillance—the Kauffman suite. What a grandiose sight! The massive double-tiered room was filled shoulder-to-shoulder with VIPs—senators, governors, mayors, the baseball commissioner, etc. I observed that Mr. Kauffman, with elbows on knees, was engrossed in every pitch. I knew that this special game in this special stadium represented to him and to many others the culmination of years of time and toil and embodied substantial quantities of money.

The spacious suite, done in blue, was softly lighted by crystal chandeliers. Drinks, hors d'oeuvres, diamonds, expensive gowns—the affluence was overwhelming. It was not at all the mustard-stain ball games that I had so often pictured in dreams from the Hanoi Hilton. Ironically, this kind of baseball had been occurring for years, but ten thousand miles away I had no reason even to consider that it was happening.

Frequent introductions and small talk provided little opportunity to watch the game. The conversation was light and cordial with the common quip, "Send in Plumb," whenever the Royals' pitcher threw a ball or walked his opponent. I had occasion to silently reflect on my six years of captivity.

I felt out of place. Instead of wealth, I had known only abject poverty, not seeing so much as a humble button, much less faceted diamonds. But it was gratifying to know that, because I had tied my raveled drawstrings and had paced in battered sandals, I had in some small way helped protect this system wherein worthy individuals could attain material success. The influential people who were gathered in this suite were depicted by North Vietnamese propaganda as dangerous capitalist warmongers who exploited the poor. But as I observed their kindness and mutual respect, I knew that they were the same people who had worked hard for accomplishment and who were instrumental in programs and projects beyond their own immediate interests. As any citizen in America, they had the right to excel and to enjoy the fruits of their labors.

During the seventh-inning stretch, I was to be interviewed. On the way to the press box, I tried to anticipate questions I might be asked. The door opened, and a whispered "Shhh!" reminded me that the announcer, Buddy Blattner, was still "live." A blue cloth with a Royals emblem was hung opposite the camera as a backdrop. After the introduction, Mr. Blattner asked, "Commander Plumb, what are your impressions of the game in this elegant stadium after being gone for such a long time?"

"It's beautiful," I said. "You know, when a person is away from his home for so long a time, he has many opportunities to define what home really is. One of the things that symbolizes America is baseball because it embodies the sense of fair play, of competition, of enjoyment for enjoyment's sake, of freedom which is so uniquely a part of this country. It's really great to be home in America!"

"Great" was an understatement. Not until I had lived year after year under totalitarian domination did I learn to fully appreciate the freedoms that Americans have fought for and have won. Growing up in America provided the training grounds necessary to endure the North Vietnamese attempts at dehumanization. Even though America has made its mistakes, it still provides a means to correct them. In this nation I can assemble with others, read from a free press, criticize and hear criticism, worship as I wish, and influence the direction of my country by voting. Here I am free to hope, to dream, to succeed.

* * *

My appearance at the new Harry S Truman baseball stadium was just the prelude to vacations, an automobile, gifts, and the general red-carpet treatment of a "hero's welcome" that returning POWs have received. The truth of the matter is I don't even know how to define "hero," but I certainly don't feel that I am one. I'm very fortunate. I still have my health and am "pressing on" as if I had been gone just a few months. I have experienced what must be the ultimate in loneliness and tedium, and I have learned that these things can be surmounted. I had no "heroic" strength or ability to overcome the physical and mental torture I endured. My strength came from faith in God and love for country. These things made it possible to find freedom behind bars. I never knew the date I would be permitted to go home, but I was confident that everything possible was being done to make it happen. The prayers, letters, VIVA bracelets, concern, and support of an entire nation brought me back. There could have been no other outcome.

Six years is a long time ago, but I can still clearly recall that day when I entered a new ball park and dedicated myself to win another kind of ball game.

background

Born in Gary, Indiana, I could not yet lift my head when my parents moved to Washington State. My dad, a construction and maintenance man, then followed war work to the Sunflower Ordnance Plant and settled in Lecompton, Kansas, a small town built in the rolling hills and woodland along the Kaw River. It was a quiet place except on Saturdays when farmers came to load their pickups with feed while their wives bought the week's groceries. Lecompton's 350 residents were like one big family, and most of them met each Sunday at the town's only church and lingered after the service to talk about the weather, their crops, and the war.

But the war was too remote for me to understand. My world was one of sparrow nests, bull snakes, and big American elms to climb, and games of "kick the can" and marbles. It was a place where change was hardly noticeable, where the same water seemed to flow around the bend each day and dusty roads disappeared behind the same knolls. It

was bicycle distance to fresh country eggs, raw milk, crab apples . . . and poison ivy. Hunters bagged hearty meals of red squirrels or cottontails, and fishermen pulled thirty- and forty-pound flatheads out of the Kaw—if they spit on their hooks. Katydids droned warnings of oncoming thunderstorms moving in from the southwest. Mom always seemed to call me in just before my jar was full of lightning bugs.

After Sunday school and church, I'd run home and quickly change clothes so I could go horseback riding with Merta Lou Wingfield. We always rode double because she said the other four or five horses in the stall couldn't be ridden. Bareback, we followed the trails into the woods toward our favorite spot, an old log cabin overlooking the Kaw Valley. We lay on our backs and watched hawks soar with motionless wings. Toward suppertime Merta Lou and I returned to the barn, fed the mare its oats, and said good-bye. I picked the sticktights out of my socks and rode my bike home to eat Mom's roast beef and applesauce.

When I was about twelve I hung around with a group of older guys who took me along only because they wanted to attract my sister's attention. They were always going down to Hoad's cow pond or to the Kaw River to skinny dip. I couldn't swim, and so I would take an inner tube along and crawl around in the mud on the edge while the others went out to the middle. The boys started taking me out farther each time and finally—of necessity—I learned to swim.

I acquired a love for music at an early age. When I was in the second grade my dad bought me a trumpet for eight dollars, and I started playing in the school band and at church. By the time I was eleven I was able to play "Trumpeter's Lullaby." That was the year the older guys in high school won the football championship and asked me to play that song at their banquet.

It was a cold December night, and I had left my horn in the car while I ate. When it was about time for me to play, I brought it in. I touched the mouthpiece to my lips, and it was so cold it froze there. The valves barely moved. The accompanist started to play, but I could blow only three or four notes. It was the most traumatic experience of my young life.

The following year I started throwing the *Topeka Capital*. I had about fifty customers on a five-mile route—farther than I wanted to ride a bicycle. One day Dad and I went to the Bank of Perry, a few miles from Lecompton, and with his cosignature I became the youngest borrower in the history of the bank. I used this money to buy a motor scooter with the idea that I would pay for it with paper route earnings.

One night my folks got a telephone call from the highway patrol. I had been picked up on the highway without a license. Dad had to appear in court and was told that I shouldn't have been out there. My folks had thought I was out playing with the boys; instead I was on my way to the County Fair. I didn't make it!

I attended a church camp when I was thirteen. After the service, the minister asked those present if they wanted to receive Christ into their lives, so I went up to the altar. The minister spoke to me and the others who went up, and then each of us said a prayer. Although I had been going to church and Sunday school on a regular basis, it was at that point that I was old enough to understand the meaning of commitment. I consider this my first really close association with God.

I completed eight years of grade school as valedictorian of my class and had to give a speech. Then the principal handed out diplomas; it didn't take long—there were only ten of us.

In 1956 the Plumb family moved to the "big" city—

Overland Park, Kansas. It was quite a transition, leaving the simple life of Lecompton to become part of a metropolitan area of over a million people. I was determined not to be the country bumpkin bucking a complex society. I can remember thinking, Things are going to be a lot different but I'm not going to fight them.

While I was growing up I often wondered what people thought of me and how I could make a good impression. I worked hard so I would be liked. I was a proud person—proud of my family, my country, and myself—and I was proud to be a Christian.

I wondered about morals in the city. (I was really naïve in this respect.) In Lecompton nobody stayed out late, nobody stole hubcaps, and kissing girls was out of the question. I was not confident that I could adapt, but I was going to try.

The first day in Overland Park my brother Larry and I walked around until we reached a dairy about a mile from our house. Two kids on bicycles were there, and we walked right up to them and asked their names and shook their hands and said, "We're new here, and we'd like to take a look around." The kids took us over to their house and we played touch football for a while. It took a little gritting of the teeth, but I was determined to grind it out.

I was still afraid of what the moral standards in the city might be, because I felt that this could be an area in which I would not be able to adapt. I could learn to smoke, and I could probably even bear to drink beer, but when it came to sexual experimentation I decided I probably couldn't conform. My parents, never meddling, loved and trusted me. I wasn't going to disappoint them.

The kids at Milburn Junior High did things I'd never done. At Lecompton I had square danced, but I soon discovered that at Milburn it was considered "Hayseed." My sister Carol was in college by that time and knew all about dancing, so she helped me. I also took lessons from a dancing instructor.

The instructor had a daughter who was a couple of years younger than I—a potential cheerleader, homecoming queen, etc. I got to know Vicki through my dancing lessons and asked her to the junior high Christmas dance. We were cutting a wide swath around the floor, and on the last dance I directed her over to the mistletoe. At the last chord, I dipped her low, leaned her back . . . and dropped her smartly on the floor. Embarrassed, I didn't know what to do. She regained her poise, however, by sitting up and clapping along with the others. That would never have happened at a square dance.

After all the lessons from my sister and the dance instructor, I was ready for the "big time." I was on the Bandstand television program one afternoon, and as soon as I got home, I received a phone call. It was from Merta Lou. She had been watching the program and there was Chuck Plumb! I looked like a fish out of water to her because I was dressed in suit and tie and was doing all kinds of fancy footwork on television. Just a few months earlier Merta Lou and I had been "steadies."

But I wasn't "Chuck" anymore. "Chuck" or "Chuckie" wouldn't suit my new image, and so I became Charles. In high school, people started calling me Charlie; I even had my senior cards engraved "Charlie Plumb." When I brought them home, my dad said, "Every white horse in the country is named Charlie."

I remember crying just one time when I was in junior high and that was when my girl deserted me. I was going steady with Elizabeth Trout, but she moved away. We wrote for several months, and when she moved back I was afraid to stop by to see her. To this date—and a characteristic of mine—I build up an event in my mind, but when it is time to enjoy it, I back off a little for fear that it won't be as pleasant as I had imagined. That's the way it was when Liz came back. Of course she was angry and told me in no uncertain terms that we were through. It took the eight blocks home to dry my eyes.

In junior high I played the trumpet in the band and orchestra. I also tried out for a play and got the part. I kept driving myself to adapt, trying hard to become a city person.

I was still small, only 5'2", when I enrolled in high school, Shawnee Mission North. This size and another standard teen-age problem—pimples—made me self-conscious, but I wasn't going to let these stop me. I found out early that my athletic ability was going to be totally on an intramural scale (church basketball, etc.). I did do well in gym because I knew the basics; I even established a new sit-up record in that class. I tried out for the swimming team and made it with the breaststroke until a foreign exchange student from Norway showed up. He was one moving breaststroker, and he took my spot.

I continued to devote my time and efforts to music and drama. I changed from the trumpet to French horn, played in the band and orchestra, and was a member of several ensembles. I was in six plays during high school and had the lead in several of them. In one of the plays, *Balcony Scene,* the cast received a rating of "1" in the state contest.

I joined the flying club at Shawnee Mission, but I couldn't do much more than watch the other boys build their planes because I didn't have enough money to buy the expensive models. I was paying fifteen dollars a month on my scooter and trying to impress Liz Trout with cokes and 45 rpm records. I did build one plane but was reluctant to take my .049 out when the other guys had fancy .35 Cubs.

During one of the first high school meetings, a basketball coach, Bob Johnson, told us how he had flown off carriers during World War II and how important it was to land on the first try. I thought, Man, that would be the life, but I could never make it. Even as a senior I somehow felt limited. All my buddies were doing it, so I too planned to go to K.U. or K. State and work for a degree in electrical or nuclear engineering. I knew nothing about the military, and even after graduation I was not aware that the Army-Navy game was played between West Point and Annapolis.

On weekends I often drove forty miles to Lawrence where my sister Carol was attending classes at the University of Kansas. At that time she was dating Duane DeWerff, who had received a Naval ROTC scholarship and was commander of the corps his senior year. Duane gave me a booklet about the NROTC program and suggested I apply for the scholarship.

I really wanted the scholarship because I'd seen my parents sacrifice for so many years and I wasn't going to drain off any more of their hard-earned money. It didn't occur to me to apply for a loan; instead, I figured I had one of two choices: get a scholarship or forget about college. Nonetheless, getting into the NROTC program looked pretty tough.

On the last page of the booklet was this paragraph: "Qualifications for the United States Naval Academy are the same as for Navy ROTC. If you would like more information, please write . . ." So I wrote, and soon I received brochures from Annapolis.

About that time Congressman Newell George, Sixth District, Kansas, made a presentation at our school assembly. Afterward I saw him in the hall, and I thought that it would really be neat to talk to him. But what did I have to talk about? I remembered the Academy: "Congressman George, I'm Charlie Plumb, and I've been wondering about your academy appointments. Do you have any left?"

"Well, I don't have any Air Force appointments, but I still have some West Point and some Navy. How about writing my office? I'll fill you in on the details."

So I wrote once more and received instructions to take an exam in Kansas City, Kansas. I was already taking college entrance and NROTC examinations, so I thought one more test wouldn't hurt. I got up early one Saturday eager to do well on the test, and I found that about forty other fellows had the same aspirations. After I had finished, however, the state schools seemed more likely.

Several weeks later I rode the bus home from school and found a telegram on the kitchen table. It was from Congressman George:

CONGRATULATIONS. YOU HAVE JUST BEEN APPOINTED PRIMARY CANDIDATE FOR THE U.S. NAVAL ACADEMY. PLEASE SEND TELEGRAM OF ACCEPTANCE.

Underneath the message was a note from Dad, written with the first thing he could find—a green crayon.

Congratulations, son. I know you really wanted this.

Dad

The wonderful news had to be told. I rushed to the telephone and called my steady girl friend. "Hey, Anne, I've got to buy a new shirt. Do you want to go with me and help pick it out?"

"Sure."

"OK. I'll be right over."

I arrived in my white '57 Ford and laid the telegram on the front seat beside me. I opened her door, let her in, and by the time I got in she was in tears. I put my arm around her and said, "Can't you be happy for me? This is my big opportunity."

"It will be many years now before we can be together."

That was a sad afternoon. We had already made plans to go to K.U., and although both of us were seventeen, we were getting serious.

Our relationship had started several months earlier when I was working at a swimming pool as assistant manager. I had been in a water fight with some girls and ended up in a doctor's office with a scratched eye.

The next day our school band started practicing for the first football game only a month away. The "big man on campus" sauntered into the band room in white Bermuda shorts, tennis shoes, sunburned nose, and eye patch. I made my way to the French horn section and sat down in the first chair. I looked around and saw my three buddies, Roger Pilley, Jim Fleming, and Dick Hite, take first chair in their sections. The fearsome foursome were finally seniors and could "take over" the band.

We played an hour and it was break time. First chair trumpet player Dick Hite and I went out for a coke. He asked, "Boy, did you see that blonde? What do you think of her?"

"What blonde? I didn't see any blonde."

"The one playing the French horn." He pointed and said, "There she is—that one."

She was good-looking all right, but she seemed aloof. When I went back I boldly introduced myself. One thing led to another, and I said, "Do you have a ride home?"

"No."

"Well, Anne, how about letting me take you home?"

So we got into my hot, supercharged, purple and white

'55 Kaiser, but Anne wasn't impressed. She was a real door-hugger. I pulled out of the parking lot and asked, "Where do you want to go?"

"Home."

"Well, we can stop by and see a show."

"Home."

"How about a coke?"

"Home!"

I found out that Anne had been filled in on Charlie Plumb because her directions home indicated that she lived down the street from one of my best friends, Jeannie Maxwell, who had worked with me in Junior Achievement. We were just about to the top of a hill a half-block from Anne's house when my roaring Kaiser spit twice, chugged once, and died.

So now what? "I guess we get out and push," I said. Anne walked back to the right rear bumper while I stayed on the driver's side, and we started pushing the car over the hill. When we reached the peak, the car began to roll down the other side, and I jumped in to see if I could start it. By this time, the car was in front of her house. I was driving, Anne was pushing, and her whole family was out in the front yard watching. Anne yelled, "Hey, let's go in the house." I put on the brakes, raised my eye patch, and said, "No. I'll see you later."

What a debut!

It wasn't like me to date a girl who wouldn't at least let me put my arm around her. But Anne was that way, and I couldn't understand it. Just before lunch I walked her down the hall on the way to the cafeteria, but as we approached the telephone, she'd say, "Go on ahead and save me a seat." She did this every day. I knew that she was calling her mother, but I didn't know why.

Anne in Ohio and I in Kansas had participated as juniors in state music festivals, and we'd both received "2" ratings in the French horn solo division. Each of us started working in November on new music to see if we could do better.

One afternoon she asked me if she could borrow my tape recorder. She said it would help her with her practice. I took it over to her house, set it up, and gave her one of my tapes. A few days later, she said she was through with it and that I could stop by to pick it up. When I got it home, I realized that I now had two tapes. Curious, I put the second tape on the recorder, hoping to hear how my competition was progressing on her solo.

Instead of music, a voice sounded: "Happy Birthday, Anne. I would like to sing you a song. 'Happy birthday to you, happy birthday to you . . .' " After the song was over, the voice said, "Just remember that I'm thinking about you all the time and that we'll be together soon. All my love, Bart."

The next day was the big showdown. As soon as I saw Anne, I said, "OK. What's the story on Bart?"

"Well, Bart and I are in love, and we're going to get married."

"That's just wonderful. He's clear over on the East Coast and you're here. That's a long way to be in love."

It all began to fall in place. I'd been dating Anne three months and still had not kissed her, and every day she had been calling her mother to find out if she had received a letter from Bart.

I asked, "So he's coming here for Christmas, is he?"

"Yes, he's coming at Christmas. We're going to get married."

"When?"

"Well, we're going to set a date when he comes."

"What makes you think he's going to travel a thousand miles to see his sweet little Kansas girl?"

"You don't even know what love is, you country hick. I know he's coming."

"What do you want to bet? . . . How about this—if he comes, I promise I won't bother you anymore. But if he doesn't, then you and I will go steady. Is that a deal?"

"That's a deal."

December came, and we continued to practice our solos. As the days passed, Anne's face reflected her feelings. "I think you're going to win," she said.

Christmas came, but Bart didn't. I gave Anne my class ring, she put it on a chain around her neck, and I kissed her.

It was nearing music festival, and the big French horn blowoff was about to begin. I was still in first chair and Anne was in third, but I knew she was a better player. Because I had seniority in the band, though, she had to sit down the row. The local contest was first, and we both passed. A month later were the regionals, and again we passed. The band members started murmuring back and forth, "How's it going to work out?"

Finally, the day came, and all the musicians who had passed regionals rode the bus down to Emporia. Although Anne and I were steadies, there was no compromise in this contest. By late afternoon, the judges' sheet was posted on the bulletin board. Wildly, Anne and I scanned the results.

"Charlie, we both got ones!"

It was fate. We were meant for each other.

* * *

I had never been away from home for more than a week's stay at Boy Scout camps; the only military drill I had known was in a marching band. Nervously, I said good-bye to my family and Anne and left for Annapolis.

I found that I knew more than I thought. My Scouting experience came back to me because the first week was one of tying knots, boating, shooting rifles, and getting used to a uniform. I was amazed to see how much further ahead I was than fellows who had not been Scouts.

I became a member of the drum and bugle corps and the Naval Academy orchestra. Later, I became deeply involved in activities, chairing dance and social committees. I helped design the crest for our class ring. I became photography editor for the yearbook and newspaper. I spent so much time in the darkroom that I had little left for study.

Classmates were getting the expected Dear Johns because of prolonged separation. Anne wrote a letter every day, however, and when I came home for Christmas she was waiting for me at the airport. As soon as she saw me, she broke out with hives. Her entire body began to swell; her belt cut into her waist, and her socks cut into her ankles. We had barely said hello when I had to take her home.

The next night she felt better and we went to a restaurant. This time we were together for about an hour before she started breaking out again. We didn't know what it was, but as long as I stayed away from her, she was all right. For six weeks she was hospitalized to take allergy tests. With no positive returns, she finally went to a psychiatrist and was told she was allergic to a Plumb. Three months later I came home for spring break. This time everything went well.

My junior year Anne and I liked each other well enough to plan our marriage, and she decided to move to Washington, D.C. We were together every weekend. I had maintained the Superintendent's List regularly during my sophomore year, but when Anne came, my grades toppled. I have never regretted it, though, because it was such a treat to have her with me.

During June Week of my senior year, Anne and I became engaged. I received my diploma on 3 June, and twenty-three hours later we were married.

* * *

I had been active in Youth Fellowship and Youth for Christ when I was in high school and had sung in church choirs, but I was never on any church membership roll. While I was at the Academy, I continued my Christian worship. I joined the Officers' Christian Union, which prepared men to act as lay leaders on some of the Navy's smaller ships because chaplains could not be assigned to those vessels. On Easter, 1964, I was baptized.

Anne and I had been regular in church attendance while we were courting. After we were married, Anne taught Sunday school. My time was so limited, however, that I was not able to become as involved as she.

Flight training was first. I still wasn't sure if I was capable of fulfilling what would be demanded of me. I was going to be a hard charger, and instead of taking the usual thirty-day leave, I took only twelve days for our honeymoon. We left for Pensacola, Florida, immediately after we were married. I have since regretted that decision.

Flight training was exhausting, but I finally completed the jet syllabus. On 19 November 1965, I received what I thought I could never achieve—my Navy wings of gold.

For several reasons I never thought about flying the F4 Phantom. Thinking of it left a bad taste in my mouth because I had seen one crash on the *Constellation* during my midshipman cruise. I was only eighty feet away, and I saw two critically injured men being carried from the flight deck on a stretcher. They were still alive. The pilots had drowned.

Then my assignment was handed to me: F4-B Phantom. The more I learned about the bird the more I liked it. Anne and I picked up our gear and moved to San Diego, California.

It was a storybook marriage, with never so much as an argument. She was working most of the time, and on weekends we puttered in our garden and took trips.

For two and one-half years we shared a very close relationship. It was difficult to leave her and climb aboard the aircraft carrier for places unknown. The *Kitty Hawk* sailed out of port on 5 November 1966, Anne's birthday.

The night before, Anne and I walked along the streets of San Diego. I was able to sneak into a music store and order an organ that I knew Anne liked, but she came in before I had completed my instructions to the salesman. Wanting to add a special surprise to the gift, I stopped at a filling station and called back.

"This is Lieutenant J. C. Plumb. I was just in your store and bought an electronic organ from you. Tomorrow is my wife's birthday and I wonder if you could put a big red ribbon around it."

"I'll do better than that; I'll send her a bouquet of flowers."

"OK, send the bill to me on the ship but take the organ to our house. If you will, put a card on it that says, 'Love, Charles.' "

"We'll be happy to do that, sir. You're going to war, and we'll do everything we can."

Three months passed, and I still hadn't received the bill for the flowers. I was beginning to wonder what had happened, and in a telephone conversation I asked Anne, "Did you ever get the flowers I sent you with that organ?"

Surprised, she said, "Oh, no! That was the most disappointing thing in my life. I saw the organ and knew you had bought it for me, and when I opened the card pinned to the flowers, I read, 'Compliments of the Federal Music

Company.' I just broke down and cried because I thought the flowers were from you."

"They were, honey. The store just goofed."

Once again, Anne wrote faithfully every day. We were, of course, anxious to see each other, and on each letter she kept tab of the number of Saturday nights left until I came home. On 19 May 1967 Anne wrote a letter indicating only three more Saturday nights of separation. On the other side of the world I went to bed content to know we would soon be together.

3

capture

The phone disregarded my sleep. I answered to hear the voice of the operations officer inform me of an unexpected impending commitment by the Joint Chiefs of Staff—an alpha strike. The target: JCS-53. This surprise attack would be no trivial operation.

The clock hanging from the overhead registered 0300 hours. I rubbed my eyelids and yawned. 19 May 1967. Five more days and I would be leaving behind eleven months of a grand experience with my squadron. I'd be gripping many firm hands and bidding good-bye to squadron mates who were in a league all their own. I'd also be leaving my noble ship, the *Kitty Hawk,* for a five-month refresher course—a kind of spring training. Then I'd return to my country, my home, my wife! I'd be with Anne again! A mixture of joy and nostalgia stirred my mind.

As flight schedules officer I opened my little green memo book—affectionately referred to by my squadron mates as the "Big Wheel Book"—to begin jotting down assignments for this particular strike. It was a difficult task, because I had to keep records of all the pilots and assign to them the "good deals" and the "bad deals." It made a lot of difference: all of the pilots wanted combat missions and opportunities for more flight time. There were no "pansies"—nobody wanted the easy way out. I had to keep all of them equal in their number of flights—their combat missions, their night catapults, their test hops; these were the "good deals." The "bad deals" were assignments which involved little or no flight time—waiting for a broken bird to be repaired in Da Nang or being scheduled to stand a duty watch. I kept the book with me at all times because the pilots would constantly badger me about their slate.

"Hey, Charlie, I've got only six alphas. How about letting me in on this hop?"

"Sorry, pal. We've got enough hot rods this time. Besides you've got eight alpha strikes, and you know it."

If ever I were shot down, the memo book could provide important classified information to the enemy—names, numbers of missions, etc. So, as a precaution, I had coded each name in my squadron by assigning a three-letter designator; for example, I recorded myself as PLM. In my mind, I had prepared the answer to my mates' frequent quip, "Hey, Plumber, what are you going to do with that little book when the gooks get their hands on you?"

Denny Wisely had already shot down a MIG and a Colt. I would give him a test hop and give PLM his chance at a MIG. The eleven o'clock dental appointment would simply have to wait. My regular radar intercept officer (RIO) would be the backseater for the skipper this time, because the skipper's regular RIO had taken a small-arms slug in the shoulder and was incapacitated. Consequently I had my choice of the cream of the crop in RIOs, and I picked Denny's regular backseater, Gary Anderson.

I opened my stateroom door and entered the corridor. The *Kitty Hawk*'s night-lights, casting a magenta hue, exposed the way to the wardroom where I poured a cup of coffee and singled out a doughnut. I was pretty keyed up at this point, pressed to inform all the guys about the strike. A squadron pilot passed and dropped his hopeful hint, "I hear you've got the big one, Charlie."

"Yeah. You stay here and write your wife a letter," I winked, "for a change."

Being a junior officer, I was in a delicate situation, having to tell some of the senior people that they weren't included in this strike effort.

I finished my coffee. On the way to the ready room I noticed the early morning stillness and the eerie atmosphere produced by the night-lights. It was the lull before a storm. In the hanger bay the planes reflected ethereal purple from their tails and canopies. Peripheral waves rustled against the carrier hull like spent leaves swirled by autumn gusts.

I walked on. The pilots of the fighter planes gathered in their own briefing room and read from a television screen and teletype the weather information and position of the ship. We reviewed once again the switches we would have to throw, and I coordinated with the maintenance officer the weapons we would need, the volume of fuel, etc. Serious thoughts were in the backs of all our minds, but outwardly our mood was light. We laughed and joked, drank coffee, and smoked.

My regular RIO was up to his old habit of manipulating his slide rule. Being a self-styled math wizard, he again pinpointed his likelihood of getting "bagged"; this was based on some speculative formula he had found somewhere.

"Today, friends," he proclaimed, "my bag-factor is .019376."

"Then save me a room at the Hanoi Hilton," I threw back.

We left our ready room and entered the central briefing room where all the pilots, RIOs, and standby crews scrutinized the master plan, which included maps and photographs of the targets and intelligence reports of the enemy's fire capability. After our central briefing we returned to our ready room, meditated last-minute instructions, and put on our flight gear. Altogether, these briefings often took as long as, and sometimes longer than, the mission itself.

I looked up at the screen: . . . PILOTS . . . MAN YOUR AIRCRAFT. . . . We slapped each other on the back, exchanged the customary "Give 'em hell!" dialogue and patted the posterior of our "good luck girl" hanging on the door. It was time to go topside.

Only then—six and a half hours after I had awakened—did I discover the weather conditions that the ticker tape had already revealed. Existing for so long in the bowels of the ship and almost forgetting about the miracle of night and day, I was elated to see brilliant sunshine sparkling off the green waters of the Gulf of Tonkin. It was beautiful!

I rechecked the number of the aircraft that I would be flying and found that it was already on the catapult. Gary and I would be the first to go. Twenty yards away Denny Wisely was strapping into his F4. Above the flight deck noise he hollered, "Look, Charlie, I've got missiles aboard. How about it?"

"Sorry, Killer. You'd scare 'em all away."

"Well, if you need a spare, I'll go."

"If I need a spare, you hamburger, I'll get a retread." It

would have been foolhardy to take an untested bird into combat conditions, so I gave him the "thumbs down" to indicate disapproval.

Preparing for launch was a ritual. Enlisted men and officers in multicolored shirts scrambled to and fro, pouring gasoline and liquid oxygen into the aircraft, loading bombs and missiles, moving gear. From the tower above instructions were bellowed via bullhorn by my competent air boss, Commander Bill Russell: "Pilots are manning their aircraft for the 1030 launch. Pick up all loose gear about the decks. Reduce to three-point tie-downs. Secure your goggles; check your straps; put your sound attenuators in place."

The men hustled to finish their tasks. Gary and I shook our plane's ailerons, kicked its tires, examined its engines and missiles. Seeing no problem, we climbed the ladder and began to strap in. Commander Russell announced the time hack and updated the position of the carrier. We would have to dead reckon from this position, plotting the distance and direction in order to locate the ship on our return.

And then, just as the electrifying order at Indy—"Gentlemen, start your engines," the air boss delivered our command: "Pilots, start the jets."

I closed the canopy. The engines emitted deafening roars. The deck crew released the chains and tie-downs; and two catapult officers, with meticulous hand signals and exaggerated lip movements, directed the aircraft onto the cats.

It was mandatory that I watch the engine gauges carefully—RPM, oil, hydraulic, temperature, fuel flow, fire warnings, etc. Sequentially, I examined the fifty or so items on the checklist, corroborating with Gary on the hot mike in a low tone: "Fuel pump . . . on. Trim selector . . . on. Navigation equipment . . . on. Receiver, channel nine . . . on . . ." And so it continued until all the checks were complete. The cat officer twirled his index finger: Run 'em up! I advanced the throttles.

"Engine run-up is good. Takeoff checklist is complete. I'm ready to go. Gary, you ready?"

"Yeah, I'm ready."

"OK," I mocked. "This is your captain speaking. Welcome to Flight 403 to Hanoi, North Viet Nam. We'll be flying at an altitude of eleven grand, and we have a high ceiling. Make sure your belt is fastened. No smoking, please."

The position of the stick had to be perfect. I placed my elbow into my stomach to stifle any arm movement that would otherwise be created by the tremendous jolt of the catapult. (A month earlier, a stick wasn't exact, and an RIO—a close friend of mine—was lost when the aircraft went into the drink and he was sucked into the carrier's screws.)

Because my right hand was welded to the stick, I raised my left hand to deliver the salute to the cat officer. The salute was partly tradition—one always salutes when leaving his ship—but it was also an indication that everything looked good and that we were ready to go. It was important that I would not raise my hand to give a "thumbs down" indication nor would I bring the throttles back if I saw a last-second warning light. Even though the engines' lag time was an amazing four seconds to peak thrust, the catapult would shoot the aircraft off the deck in just three seconds, and down into the drink we'd go! The launch was no time for a cat officer to misunderstand my signal.

"OK, Gary, I'm saluting."

At that moment the cat officer, with an ostentatious sweep of the hand, dropped to one knee. A crewman pushed the button. My airplane cocked back, and the overwhelming impact of the G-force, like a carnival ride, molded my uncontrolled body to the seat. We were rocketing at 150 knots (about 170 MPH) at the end of 170 feet of flight deck! My eyes bulged as the skin around them was drawn back. Dust relayed its stinging presence to my face. Despite the force on my chest I gasped. A perfect cat shot!

My orders were to make a spiral climb to Angels 10 (10,000 feet), rendezvous with a tanker, and top off with 2,000 pounds of fuel—the amount required to replace that consumed during the start, takeoff, and climb. Refueling immediately after takeoff seemed strange, but the extra volume was very important for the return flight. As I climbed skyward, I looked down and saw the miniature carrier with its toy airplanes being shot off the catapult with a puff of steam. A destroyer bobbled up and down in the furrowed wake, watching for anyone who might drop into the water.

The tanker, an A3 "Whale," had been shot off another catapult about the same time. Carrying many more tons of fuel, it took a little longer to reach the briefed altitude. When it did, I approached it from behind, throttled back slightly, and pushed the button to extend my in-flight refueling probe. Almost instinctively I knew where the probe must be to plug into the tanker's drogue—a basket-like funnel at the end of a sixty-foot rubber tube. With deep concentration on the moving drogue I eased up and plugged in. Only then did I see what I had been staring at during the approach: on the "Whale's" tail—WE GIVE GREEN STAMPS.

With refueling completed I again throttled back, pulled out, rolled left, and ascended to eleven grand, waiting for my squadron mates to refuel. Ten minutes passed, and so had 1,000 pounds of gasoline through my engines. I decided to sneak to the back of the pack for "seconds." If I should encounter a MIG I did not want to worry about being in a prolonged dogfight with a shortage of fuel. I wanted to know that I could tap my afterburners when I needed them.

Besides, it was impossible to "dead stick" my aircraft back onto the flight deck.

All of this coordination of men and machinery during the refueling was done in complete silence—we called it "zip lip." Although enemy radar would have already detected us, we were careful not to give radio "spooks" any additional information. It was gratifying to experience such close rapport with my air wing: I knew, and they knew, what each was doing in this intricate maneuver, yet not a word had to be spoken.

The strike team, loaded with fuel, established formation. Sixteen A6 bombers flew ahead at Angels 9. Behind them and a thousand feet higher eight F4 flak suppressors grouped into their divisions. And yet another thousand feet higher were eight MIG-CAP (combat air patrol)—four at each flank. Also included in the strike were the vital tanker, rescue, and electronic counter-measures aircraft.

The flak suppressors performed a demanding function: they flew above the bombers, tapped their afterburners, and swooped down ahead of the formation to discourage antiaircraft artillery. These planes were the first ones in, and their timing was critical. They could not fly too far ahead, nor could they lag into the falling explosives released by the bombers following them down the chute.

I was one of eight MIG-CAP, positioned at the formation's extreme port side. MIGs could not successfully attack head on and would approach our flanks. Gary and I protected the flanks and helped coordinate the thirty-two aircraft in a formation which extended about three miles from side to side. As I observed this formation streaking toward the target at 500 knots, I marveled at the tremendous firepower we represented.

We drew nearer the coast, and the MIG-CAP descended to

Angels 10 and joined the flak suppressors; then the combined group dropped to Angels 9 and picked up the A6 bombers, all the while under "zip lip." We became "feet dry" at Angels 7, crossing the golden sands of the North Vietnamese beach and the flooded rice paddies enclosed in patterned embankments. I paused to think of how many of my closest buddies weren't there to see it. Instead, they had "bought the farm"—crashed and been killed or captured. I felt sorrow and even a sense of guilt, being able to fly free. (I suppose the feeling was much the same kind that families have when, after losing loved ones, they try to celebrate Christmas.)

We broke silence after we crossed over land because it was necessary for us to alert each other of oncoming MIGs and surface-to-air missiles. We flew inland until we reached the Troung Song mountain range and turned north to follow the ridgeline which shielded us from enemy missiles. From one of our big radar birds—an EC121 Super Constellation capable of screening all of North Viet Nam—came an alert: "MIGs Hanoi. Twenty West."

Gary flicked the radarscope to twenty miles west of Hanoi and picked up the two reported MIGs as they left their airfield about thirty miles away. The formation now veered right toward the target, and like an impatient youngster awaiting his birthday, I was anxious to get my crack at a MIG before I went home. Being in the outermost aircraft on the port flank I slipped even farther to the left, leaving my position to insure first encounter with the enemy. Then over my radio came the skipper's reprimand: "Lindfield Two. Pull it in." I felt humiliated at having to be told to get back where I belonged. At the same instant, electronic equipment warned me that a SAM radar antenna was sweeping our formation . . . but danger was not imminent unless the antenna "locked on." During our briefings we had prearranged to "jink" to the right on call, to maneuver wildly starboard at the skipper's command.

The call came, and the entire formation jinked to avert any oncoming missile. During my hasty visual canvass of the ground below I heard another call: "Resume." I rolled left and reassumed the flight course.

On my radarscope I could see the MIG coming—now about twenty miles away. A sudden frantic alert burst through my headphones: "MIG! Ten o'clock high!" How could that MIG get here so fast? My eyes shot up at ten o'clock. It was a Navy A6, no cause for alarm.

"Negative. It's an A6," I keyed the mike and sighed.

I was puzzled that an A6 was heading in the opposite direction of our flight. All of our A6's were still in proper formation, so I concluded that mechanical trouble had forced this one back from another strike. I should have given the unusual incident more attention, because, as I later surmised, that A6 was probably trying to jam a SAM radar antenna that had locked on my aircraft. My electronic equipment verified this with its input. But then I couldn't be jinking fancy little whifferdills all the time, because I'd run out of gas before I could get back to the "Whale." I smoothly rocked one wing and then the other.

"Gary. Do you see it?"

"I don't see a thing, Charlie."

We had both seen SAMs before. They resembled flying white telephone poles with huge Fourth of July sparklers spraying silvery-orange glows from their tails. If we saw them in time, we could dodge the missiles by letting them close in and, at the last second, pulling the plane into a high-G barrel roll—six Gs or so—and letting the poles pass harmlessly underneath. Because of its design, the missile could not follow us without cracking in two.

But we didn't see it.

Boom! I felt a thump in the empennage, the aft section of the airplane. Red instrument lights jumped across the panel, indicating that I had two engines on fire. That wasn't good—this plane had only two engines. I yanked the throttles back to idle, and the bird seemed to come to an immediate halt in midair.

"Charlie! We're hit! How bad is it?"

"She's still flyin'."

Then the aircraft started to roll; and while I madly scanned the instruments, I looked up and found that the F4 had suddenly overturned; ground was where there should have been sky, and the nose was heading downward ripping the air at 500 knots. The altimeter needle collapsed to 4000, to 3500, to 3000. We had to get out, but being inverted, we would be rocketed by the ejection seat right into the rice paddies. I had to roll the plane upright. I tried the stick. It was frozen! The only manual control was the rudder pedal, not normally used to roll an aircraft. I stepped on it as hard as I could, adrenaline surging through my veins.

The plane shuddered once, then again. Slowly it began to right itself. Rear-view mirrors reflected a screaming fire-ball—12,000 pounds of flaming gasoline and 30,000 pounds of fissionable aircraft.

"You want to eject?"

"No, wait a minute," I shouted back.

The plane struggled; the sky was where it should be.

"Gary, let's go!"

I jerked my face curtain to eject. The rocket slammed me out of the aircraft, I tumbled a couple of times, and the chute caught—just as advertised.

All kinds of debris filled the air around me as wadding from shells whistled by.

"Son of a gun, they've bagged my airplane. Now they're after me!"

I winced at the concussions from exploding shells—sonic booms battering my eardrums. Rockets of heavy smoke clouded the sky. Gary and I had ejected so near the ground, however, that enemy guns could train on us for only a short time.

I checked my parachute canopy. It looked good—torn in only a couple of places. I thought of escape. But where? Looking away, I saw my buddies and their aircraft blending into the horizon. Below, my landing zone was nothing but barren rice paddies. Down to my left, a huge cloud of black smoke billowed at the outskirts of a peasant hamlet, punctuating a row of four or five huts. My plane . . . had it wiped out a family? If so, the villagers would certainly be unhappy. I wasn't happy either—I hadn't intended that to happen. I later learned that the plane had impacted just beyond the last shack on the road.

There was precious little time before I would touch down, and much had to be done. I grabbed my two-way radio and tried to contact Gary, but I received no answer. Then I called my skipper:

"Lindfield Lead. Lindfield Lead. This is Lindfield Two. We've got two good chutes. We're going to be all right. Request no SAR effort."

Gary and I were much too far inland to expect any successful Sea Air Rescue. There was no need to get a chopper shot down with three or four men in it. We would be landing near the village and would not be able to evade for five minutes, much less the forty-five it would take for a rescue team to get there. I'd seen helicopters shot down during rescue operations for pilots who had already been killed or captured, and I would not initiate such an incident.

If I were to make it out, it would have to be unassisted.

As soon as I completed the radio transmission, I broke off the aerial, threw it one direction, and the radio the other. Then I remembered my flight schedules book! I yanked it from my pocket and started shredding the pages. I also tried gulping down bits of paper, but it was too much—fifty pages or so—and I never had been a fast eater. I ripped out pages containing unclassified information, released them, and watched them flutter away. Then I bowed my head. "Well, Lord, here I am. I'm really in a bind now, and I need some help. Give me strength, and give Anne strength."

I was surprised at how calm I was when I should have been panic-stricken. But there was too much to think about and do; I couldn't let myself become irrational. While I shredded information from my little book, I pondered the names and the experiences behind that information; it would all be different now. I tried to envision myself in this new world and prepare for it.

I had a lot going for me. I was in good physical condition and I could probably withstand torture. I didn't believe I would be killed because I was too much of a blue chip for the enemy. But what about my mind? Would it be so twisted that I would change my values and become a Communist . . . or a vegetable? I knew I'd rather die than go home that way. No! I wouldn't let that happen! But how could I resist? I'd simply have to sustain, to perpetuate my values by continually summoning and applying all the things I'd ever known. I would hang on to my faith in God and my love and respect for my country. Otherwise, I would go home a different person. No one would know me. This was my greatest fear.

Touchdown. I plunged backwards into mud and water, releasing the remaining bits of paper as I did so. Bubbles and a few shreds oozed to the surface. Trying to get my bearings, I took off my helmet and mask and crawled without direction in the quagmire. With slimy hands I tried to wipe mud from my eyes. I saw that I was about ten or fifteen yards from an embankment. I looked over to see that Gary, touching down in an adjacent paddy about one hundred yards away, had disappeared behind the eight-foot embankment.

A barefoot peasant wearing khaki shorts and T-shirt ran top speed down the path toward me, grimacing with excitement and anger. Above his head he waved a double-edged ax with blades about eight inches long. My instructors had never documented that kind of weapon!

He started to scream, "Han' up! Han' up!"

I didn't understand what he meant, and I kept working with my gear and chute. I had a .38 revolver strapped to my chest, and as long as he stayed on the embankment I would not touch it.

It wasn't long, however, before ten or twelve more peasants came rushing toward me, yelling and waving their shovels and hoes. Now there was power in numbers, and they charged out into the water after me. I raised my hands away from my body. They started ripping at my G-suit, found my survival knife, and proceeded to cut away at the suit and torso harness. I tried to tell them to use the zippers, and even attempted to show them how to do it, but they knocked my hands away.

The more certain they were that I was harmless, the meaner they became. Shovel and hoe blades flailed at my body to prove to me that I was their loathed captive. Strangely, the peasants failed to see my revolver, probably because it, too, was covered with mud; and the .38 rested in my holster at least three or four minutes before a peasant finally spotted it. He yanked it out of the holster and sloshed

a few steps away. A moment later he returned and screamed for special attention. He fixed the barrel to my head. I could see that at least two of the chambers were empty. I had always kept five of the six chambers loaded, so I knew that he must have removed at least one of the cartridges. There was little I could do as I felt the muddy barrel against my temple. The peasant pulled the trigger. Click! He guffawed and sneaked away, wiping off his unexpected prize.

Approximately thirty villagers had surrounded me by this time, clawing at my clothing until I was completely naked. They frisked me, jabbing fingers over my entire body with the hope they would claim another weapon. Satisfied that nothing remained hidden, they allowed me to put on my shorts. Then they blindfolded me with a tatter from my flight suit and tied my wrists behind my back. I thought that they were going to direct me to my molten aircraft to show me what extensive damage I had done; instead they prodded me just off the path of the embankment. I could see under my blindfold that they were purposely forcing me to stumble along on rocks and pieces of broken glass.

People emerged from all directions, brushing against me and grabbing my fingers, forcing them backwards. Try as they would, these peasants were so small that they were unable to express their fury effectively. I could counter their efforts to hurt me without feeling great pain.

Gary and his entourage had caught up with us now. As we were brought together I slurred a quick question: "You all right?"

"Yeah . . . a few burns, but I'm OK. How about you?"

"Good shape."

I knew Gary well enough to know that he must have been severely burned, probably from the ejection, or he would not have mentioned it. He was the type of guy who said he was fine when he wasn't. As soon as the peasants discovered that we had been talking, they cudgeled us with their shovels to separate us. I didn't see Gary again until we checked in at the Hanoi Hilton.

The peasants led me to a holding pen for one of their water buffalo. They thrust me past the gate and prodded the beast in an effort to make it charge and gore me. The buffalo was so docile, however, that its grazing horns drew no blood.

Ultimately, the peasants escorted me into their school-house, a large single-room structure, and tied me to a rough-hewn wooden post. Apparently, the village chief had decided it would be best to limit my vision, because the men soon gathered irregular boards and stacked them around me. It was a fruitless endeavor: I easily saw that fifteen or twenty little children were peeking through the cracks. I teased them a little by slumping motionlessly and then suddenly jerking my head toward them. Startled ooh's and aah's spilled from their mouths as they leapt back.

On the wall opposite me a blackboard preserved the day's lesson. Instead of the usual grade school numbers and letters, accurate silhouettes of American aircraft had been carefully reproduced. Would this be the material for tomorrow's test? And what kinds of answers about me would these children recite? Would PLM be as hard for them to define as these alien surroundings were for me? And would I be able to brace myself for this new world, this "away game," not even knowing its rules?

Caked mud cracked off my arms as the heat intensified. It must have been about noon, I thought. By then the dental assistant on the *Kitty Hawk* would have given up waiting and would have gone to the ward room, convinced that I was just another cocky "jet jock" too afraid to face the dentist's drill.

My mouth was dry.

torture

Uniformed soldiers arrived and were obviously content to find me blindfolded, gagged, and stripped down to shorts. My arms and shoulders throbbed from the restraints at the elbows behind my back, and at the wrists in front. Promptly, the guards disentangled the bast from the support and flung me onto the flatbed of their Russian-made jeep.

By manipulating my eyebrows and forehead, I found that I could steal glimpses at the alien surroundings. The blindfold—or what the Vietnamese called a blindfold—was nothing more than an old rag through which I could see that sharp pieces of metal—mostly junk—and a wrench or two were the sources of the jabs in my torso. Two guards were in the front, joking and laughing. One drove, and the other rode "shotgun" with an AK-47 automatic rifle on his lap. Trucks frequently roared by, and I could hear that another jeep was in front of me. I wondered if its cargo was my copilot Gary Anderson, and my concern for his severe burns returned.

The greater the lapse of time, the more remote was the possibility of escape. I pried the outside world to define my location. Unobtrusively forcing my arms and wrists, I discovered that the bindings could be loosened enough to permit some freedom. Just a little more twisting, and one hand would be free! In my mind, a wrench at my feet became a potential weapon. I looked up. The oblivious guards continued to relish their newly acquired captive. Could I possibly subdue them and take the jeep? Perhaps. But what then? A darted glance informed me that distant mountains to my left meant that we were northbound, probably toward downtown Hanoi, a mere half hour away.

Where would I run for cover? Where could I take the jeep? Just off the road ankle-deep water flooded the newly planted rice paddies. Five hundred yards distant a thin row of trees shaded the banks of an irrigation stream. Behind the trees were more rice paddies. This was typical delta terrain, broken only by the irregular silhouettes of mountains on the horizon. The road was actually a levee, elevated three or four feet to provide access for vehicles and to contain the waters. Every few seconds the jeep passed a North Vietnamese peasant plodding along the road's apron.

The farther the guard drove the more populated the area became, until the roadway seemed to be constrained by a solid wall of people. Assessing the possibility of escape realistically—no cover, no direction to run or drive even if I could overcome the guards and take the jeep, knee-deep mud and water to the nearest trees—I decided my chances were nil. I made the loosened ropes appear unmolested.

On the way the jeep stopped two or three times, and at each point were crowds, especially children. One of the stops was at a school, and I heard youngsters screaming with excitement. A guard removed my blindfold, and I discovered that these children were inquisitive, almost anxious, to see an American. A curious mixture of boldness and apprehension was manifested whenever a singular child would risk touching me. The children were not at all hostile until the guards taught them how to react properly: they must shake their fists and throw dirt clods and rocks. The mystery became the monster, and little hands groped for the nearest stone or stick.

During my imprisonment I saw again and again the almost unbelievable influence Communist officials had over the Vietnamese people. At the snap of a finger, docile civilians could be turned into angry mobs, spitting and screaming and hitting me so vehemently that the guards would have to step in to control the throng in order to avert serious injury.

Paramount in my mind during the entire trip was the impulse to escape. I tried to remember everything—directions, road signs, the name of the school, license plates, bizarre buildings, crossroads, knolls, everything. This super-sensitivity to the environs could be valuable if I were to escape. My mind boggled at the profusion of sights and sounds normally so mundane but now so important.

The trip into downtown Hanoi, including the stops, took approximately two hours during which the tarpaulin sealed in the broiling heat of the early afternoon sun. My mouth started to cotton, but a merciful passing thundershower provided a brief respite. My concentration on details allotted no time for me to realize the jostle my body encountered from the scrap metal and tools, and only after I saw my many scratches and bruises did I comprehend the aberrant journey over rough dirt roads. People were everywhere, and bicycles—thousands of them. Huge billboards portrayed jingoistic North Vietnamese waving flags and aiming rifles toward U.S. aircraft. Dirt-encrusted debris veneered the streets between rows of mud and tar paper shacks.

As the jeep slowed at a corner, I glanced up to see a drab white monolithic wall about eighteen feet in height with brown stone offsets at twenty- to thirty-foot intervals. (I had to preserve the guards' trust by acquiescing to a slumped position with my head bowed.)

The vehicle turned and slowly ascended a ramp toward a small opening in the wall—too small, I thought, to provide passageway. It stopped. A heavy iron gate opened, accompanied by the dissonant clanking of chains on metal. The jeep moved a few feet forward, again accompanied by clanking. When it stopped, I was in complete darkness. More clangor, and another gate opened, revealing a broadening shaft of light at the opposite end of the tunnel. We entered a courtyard of approximately twenty-five by forty yards, enclosed by two-story buildings of off-white and rust-spotted stucco walls with green doorframes and overhangs. Laundry hung casually from the many iron-barred windows, and rickety ladders were suspended from small balconies. Inside the courtyard, two well-kept gardens (plots of twenty by thirty-five feet containing rosebushes, camelias, and dwarf trees) were elevated to about knee level. This time there were no children—only armed guards.

My assumption was correct. Gary was held captive in the jeep ahead of mine. At the instant I recognized Gary, I started calling hysterically for a doctor to attend to his burned arms. The guards restrained me violently, screaming foreign but distinct warnings to attempt no more communication. I did, however, shout one more thing—I don't know why unless it was for morale: "These people are a thousand years behind in blindfolds!" (Later the POWs who were in nearby cells and heard me still laughed about this.)

Guards paraded Gary in front of the garden patch, which turned out to be the camp showplace for Vietnamese and foreign dignitaries. Two or three motion-picture cameras whirred, and several still cameras clicked. Gary was shoved back into his jeep; then the guards cut my leg ropes and shoved me to the same spot. I wasn't at all happy about having pictures taken by these North Vietnamese photographers, so I assumed a dramatic pose for them by extending the middle finger of both hands. I don't know whether these pictures ever got back to the States, but I intended to let all viewers know that my visit to this infamous hotel was anything but cordial. Doubtless, these films were important to the North Vietnamese officials, however, because Gary and I represented propaganda prizes—gifts from the militia to its revered uncle Ho Chi Minh on his birthday, 19 May. I wondered if he would see the pictures and understand my graphic message. I hoped so!

My lessons in a long course on Vietnamese propaganda techniques were just beginning. The prominence of official billboards, newspaper articles, posters, and banners with lettering ten feet in height announced new tallies of shot-down American aircraft. It seemed that the North Vietnamese welcomed our bombing because it increased their opportunities to correct the banners and replace the headlines with still higher numbers of "kills." These statistics provided a rallying point which government officials used to get the support of their constituency. They never mentioned, of course, that a power plant was leveled, or that the city would be without rail transit, or that the major bridge had been razed for three months. Rather, wild emphasis was given to the victorious conquest of one more airplane and two more pilots. In their eagerness to raise the score zealous propagandists tended to have problems keeping an accurate account of the number of "kills." Any airplane spotted with smoke trailing or seen disappearing over the horizon was a legitimate tally. My aircraft must have been counted at least four times.

The picture session finally ended, and I was led to what I learned was the "New Guy Village" area and into what was to be one of several torture cells in the prison, the Green Knobby Room—so called because the walls and ceiling were covered with gobs of plaster the size of golf balls which looked somewhat like mud-dauber nests. These globs had a particular function—acoustics . . . to muffle human sound.

Two or three hours passed. I had been thrown on the floor and left to wait and wonder. Determined to find a means of escape, I noted the unusual lights at the corners of the ceiling. These were box-like contrivances with two lenses directed to the floor. Expecting all sorts of hocus-pocus, I assumed the lights were cameras of some kind, focused to record whatever I might be doing. I looked up, "shooting the bird" in case Ho Chi Minh didn't get the message the first time. (Later, I found that behind these lenses were nothing more than innocent light bulbs.)

Tangled ropes and electrical wire lay on the floor. Thinking that these might come in handy, I rolled them up into a tight ball and secured them with wire and string under the table close to the door. At the far corner of the table rested a tin bowl. A barred window above the door caught my attention, and I climbed on part of the doorframe to peer out. The perimeter wall of the camp loomed over me, casting a portentous shadow over the bars. Oddly, a tree grew near the cell entrance, so near in fact that a few branches extended through the window between the bars. A way to escape? Probably not. More likely it would provide fresh greens for chow.

Some of the green knobs on the ten-by-fourteen-foot walls had been broken off, leaving small holes. I couldn't imagine how they had been fragmented that way. Were they bullet holes? Later, I learned that they had been shattered from the impact of prisoners thrown against the walls by guards.

The mental strain caused by the urgency to escape and the accompanying insecurity in not knowing how finally surrendered to a gnawing thirst. I went to the door and called to anyone whose attention I could draw to give me water; there was no response. At last I told someone that I had to go to the bathroom, and a guard unlocked the cell. I saw a faucet and broke into a desperate run. Careless of the consequences, I gulped water until a guard knocked me to the ground, but at least my thirst was slaked. (At the time, I didn't realize that the Vietnamese do not drink tap water because it is always polluted. That would have been the least of my concerns.)

* * *

Sunset. I had difficulty seeing what was beyond my cell, so I began reminiscing about that world of active life I had loved so much. Outside, my every minute had been filled. Outside, I had been the king of the skies. Outside, I had been continually learning, doing, accomplishing. I had been proud—so very proud.

And now I was so tired . . . so perplexed . . . so confined . . . so very lonely. The trauma of overwhelming change caused my mind to reel with disorientation. I was afraid. I stared at the emptiness. Shadows crept up the walls, gradually becoming more pronounced. Curiously, a vague ghostlike impression materialized. This image took the appearance of the Master with arms outstretched—a symbol.

It was strange, yet something I felt I should expect.

I began to utter the first lines of the twenty-third Psalm:

> The Lord is my Shepherd; I shall not want.
> He maketh me to lie down in green pastures:
> He leadeth me beside the still waters.
> He restoreth my soul;
> He leadeth me in the paths of righteousness for his
> name's sake.

I repeated it aloud several times—not because of any deep religious drive but because it simply seemed the thing to do. I guess I felt that the folks back home would be disappointed if I didn't. This was in my script . . . Charlton Heston would do this in a movie. I recalled the time in junior high school when a hypnotist asked me to be one of his subjects. A lamp was supposed to turn into a hula girl, and I was supposed to go over and dance with it. Under the hypnotic "spell," I knew it was a lamp, but I danced anyway, knowing everyone would be disappointed if I didn't. I couldn't spoil the party, could I?

So I said the Twenty-third Psalm, and then I prayed. I considered making a deal with God, but rejected the idea. I made no big promises, and asked for no miracles—just strength to endure the hardship, and strength for my wife Anne. It would be difficult for her too. "Yea, though I walk through the valley of the shadow of death . . ." That was certainly where I was!

* * *

The door was unlocked, and three officers took their seats at a table covered with an azure cloth. They were followed by six or eight guards who straggled in and lined the back wall. Now it would start. I would say nothing but name, rank, serial number, and date of birth. No more!

Facing me was an older man with small-rimmed

spectacles; his military uniform bore no rank. At his left was a junior officer who would soon speak "English." The third, a man dressed in civilian clothes, was fat and well fed. (Military men could sometimes be distinguished by their little green "Soupy Sales" hats with insignias of metal gold stars on red backgrounds.)

"We read copy regulations. You obey. You live no trouble. OK?"

I did not respond.

"First regulation: You answer all question!"

The way that the North Vietnamese justified torture was peculiar. When they asked me questions and wanted military answers, I was not *tortured* to answer questions but *punished* for disobeying camp regulations.

"What airplane you fly?"

"I'm sorry. I can't tell you."

I was trying to show as much courtesy as I could to avoid his getting riled. The junior officer ordered my parachute and a loose-leaf booklet to be brought in. The book, about twenty-five pages thick, contained checklists and procedures for my aircraft.

"Here book. You name. You airplane. F4. Now, what airplane you fly? Lam Lam, what airplane you fly?"

I at first had some difficulty understanding the broken English. The translator rolled his *r*'s and pronounced the letter *i* as a long *e*. The word "live" sounded like "leave," and when I was asked, "You want leeve?" I misunderstood and thought I would be excused from the room. I was wrong. Not until weeks later did I learn what *Lam* (pronounced *Lum*) meant. *Lam* was not an obscenity—it was my Vietnamese name. I had been stripped of every material possession, and now I was to suffer the ultimate humiliation of not being able to answer to my own real name.

"Lam, what airplane?"

To answer this question was, of course, not by "my rules."

"I'm sorry. I can't answer that."

The officer again reminded me about the punishment for disobeying camp regulations.

"OK. You talk me, or you talk steel."

"Bring it on."

The two higher ranking officials left. The remaining officer with one word ordered the guards forward. They "brought it on."

The steel mentioned by the interrogator consisted of iron manacles, shackles, and a leg bar. The manacles were a rounded ⚭ hinged on one end to a rounded ⚮. At the opposite end, matching threaded holes were made wherein a screw could be placed. The shackles were cylindrical iron bars, shaped like horseshoes but rounded at the ends so that the five-foot leg bar could be slipped into them and locked. The prisoner's ankles could then be forced through the openings and secured by the bar.

The junior officer walked out. Guards blindfolded me, forced my wrists behind my back, and placed the opened jaws of the manacles around them. These had obviously been intended for the more modest Vietnamese arms: they were so small that they had to be forced together just so the screw could be seated in the bottom threads. With what looked like a roller skate key, a guard began to turn the screw. My skin was pinched between the metal and quickly succumbed to the vice. I screamed in agony. Surely the guards wouldn't get these things much tighter! Blood oozed down my hands, and still the guard kept turning the key. Like powerful magnets, the iron was finally set flush. Circulation stopped. My hands burned grayish-blue, tingled, and became numb.

A guard then wrapped a rope—first around my left elbow and then my right—and drew my elbows together behind my back. Shoulder muscles writhed, and I feared that my sternum would separate. I gasped for air.

Then I was thrown abruptly to the floor. Shackles were jammed around my ankles, and the leg bar was fastened and padlocked. Electric wire, similar to the kind that I had hidden under the table, was brought forward. I thought that the guards were going to use this to shock me, but—typical of the Vietnamese—they didn't have anything else to use for rope and had torn the wire from some light fixtures. This became the "apparatus" to wrap me up. It was first tied to the manacles, then thrown over my shoulder, and at last secured to the shackles around my ankles. Guards forced a bamboo pole under the wire and started rotating it so that the wire contracted, bringing my wrists up high on my back and drawing my face completely to my ankles. I was a human pretzel, a teacup with arms for the handle and the rest of my distorted body for the bowl.

Circulation was impaired throughout my limbs, making them extremely painful to the touch. The guards, apparently drugged, exhibited wide and glassy eyes. They maliciously kicked me in the sides, the limbs, the back, and the head, giggling and having a great time. They picked me up a few feet from the floor and dropped me. Since I was on my side most of the time, they especially enjoyed standing on my head, symbolically victorious. The rubber-tire sandals tore at my ear.

My face, a ready target for abuse, was repeatedly subjected to fisticuffs and kicks. I remember staring at the floor and seeing my tears drop into pools of blood coming from my nose. The louder I screamed, the more they flailed.

After about an hour the junior officer returned.

"You talk now?"

"Yes."

The guards loosened the wire and ropes. Blood rushed back into my veins with knifing pain.

"What airplane you fly?"

I hesitated a moment and thought, Well, they know what airplane I'm flying and so it's ridiculous to undergo such torture for information they already have.

"The F4-B."

"OK. What next target you airwing?"

"I don't know. I don't have an answer to that question."

The officer left, and again the guards approached to "talk steel." My abused ears were really bothering me, and I became concerned that my eardrums would rupture because of the sharp blows. However, the guards had apparently been instructed not to inflict permanent injury, or I'm sure that they would have directed their buffetings to my kidneys and groin. The guards also seemed to recognize my limit of consciousness and would not let me black out. I tried to knock myself out by banging my head against the tile floor, but due to the limited movement, I could not. I feigned unconsciousness. The guards responded by beating me until I groaned.

Earlier, in that outside world where I and other pilots flew sorties over targets, each of us knew that, if we were ever captured, we would never relinquish information under torture. We would die first. Now, unfortunately, death was not one of the choices. I wanted to die, but they wouldn't let me.

Around the courtyard in a nearby room, my copilot Gary Anderson was undergoing about the same treatment. As soon as I heard him exploding obscenities I knew he was near.

"Hey, Gary, you all right?" I called.

The guards were on top of me immediately, kicking and striking. Gary heard me and yelled back. It was four years later that I came across a POW who had been in a cell close to ours at the time. He said, "Boy, that was one of the craziest things I'd ever heard—you yelling, 'Hey, Gary, are you all right?' Bang. Crunch. Thud. 'Fine. How about you?' Smack. Crash. Crack."

It was unprofitable for Gary and me to continue our conversation.

The junior officer entered and started the questioning once more.

"Where next target? Where you bomb next?"

The fact was I really didn't know. The final mission was a last-minute decision. I couldn't know the answers to these questions . . . and I wasn't for a third "wrap-up," so I started telling lies, knowing full well that the answers would be cross-checked with Gary's.

"Our next target is your brewery here in Hanoi."

"Why you bomb beer factory?"

"We want to break your morale."

The officer was pleased with this information and quickly jotted my confession in his record book.

When they asked for information about the other men in our squadron I remained silent.

"Well, you friend Gareth (Gary's real name) give us answer. Now, who intelligence officer? What his name?"

"Sorry. I don't know."

"OK. We know. Lt. Brooks."

The intelligence officer's first name was Brooks. Not a bad idea, I thought—giving first names as surnames. I started doing the same thing, hoping Gary would continue. He did, but as I was doing, he used the hit-and-miss lie technique as well. Fortunately, the answers were not checked that closely.

It was getting late and I was totally exhausted and intensely thirsty. The officers attempted to bribe me into answering questions by offering me water. I told a few more lies and finally was handed a cup of water. I gulped it down so eagerly I didn't realize how hot it was until I had scalded my tongue! The guards laughed. Papers were shuffled. I was given orders to remain seated on the stool in front of the questioning table. My blindfold was removed, and the men left.

My throbbing back ached for support. I started inching the stool backwards toward the interrogation table, keeping my eyes on the door in order to anticipate the guard. My elbows found the table; I leaned back and nodded into semiconsciousness.

Promptly, the guard peeked into the cell and planted the butt of his rifle into the side of the door.

"Lam Lam—unh unh unh!"

Knowing no English, he communicated with narrow eyes and pointed fingers to the stool.

"Lam, unh unh!"

My elbows fell from the table. He was not going to let me sleep. When I heard the guard's footsteps diminish to silence, I turned and looked at the much-needed back support. Cuts which I had incurred for "disobeying camp regulations" had oozed into the nice blue tablecloth! Two pools of scarlet proof. I froze. Had the guard seen it? What would they do to me now?

I could hear nothing. I rubbed one of the spots, hoping somehow that it would disappear, but I just made it worse. I looked back at the door. Still no sound. Tiptoeing on my bare feet and hunched because of my tortured back, I looked out. No one was near. I returned to the table, grabbed the opposite side of the cloth, and reversed it so that the blood stains were on the other side. Some blood had exuded through, but at least it was not on my side. No footsteps. What a relief!

The civilian official came back. He needed more answers to a few more questions.

"How you run from MIG airplane?"

I gave him a real line, knowing by this time that I could lie and get by with it. I explained some detailed wild maneuvers. When he left, I asked a favor.

"How about letting me sit or lie down on the floor so that I can sleep?"

"OK."

"One more request. How about turning off the lights?"

Although the intensity wasn't third degree, the lights did give much illumination; and because I was so tired, my eyes burned as though I had spent the night in a smoke-filled room.

"OK."

He walked out of the cell and I lay on the tile and concrete floor. I waited for the room to get dark, but it never did. Whether the officer was just kidding me or whether he forgot to turn them off, I don't know, but the lights kept burning. And so did my eyes.

Shortly thereafter the guard made his round to my cell and saw that I was on the floor.

"Lam Lam, unh unh!"

I tried to explain that the interrogator had allowed me to lie on the floor. It was no use. The guard entered the cell, struck me a few more times, and I returned to the stool.

This was the prelude to a real problem. None of the guards knew English, and no matter what I did, I could not make them understand. Countless beatings would be forth-coming because of my inability to communicate to the guards the many promises the officers made.

In the wee hours of the morning, the guard checked on me less frequently. My wrists, still in manacles behind my back, kept me off balance enough to thwart my attempts to doze. Suddenly I remembered a trick my mother used to perform. Agile when she was younger, she would hold on to her hands and, like a hoop, bring them all the way around her body without releasing them. I was in an unmaneuverable position, and the procrustean manacles allowed little motion, but I strained, and to my surprise was able to drag one foot, then the other, through.

The Green Knobby Room lacked a latrine, and so I was greatly troubled when I needed to relieve myself. Recalling the earlier incident when I had rushed for the faucet I knew I would have no second chance. The rice bowl in the corner must provide the necessary container. I urinated in it. Where could I dump it? I grew apprehensive. I felt an overwhelming need to dispose of it quickly. Where? How?

In my fear I took a sip of it . . . then another. I couldn't take any more. I went to the door and poured it under the crack. Whether I had complete control or reason at this time or hallucinations I don't know. Some of these things seem very weird now.

At last I sank to the floor. My agony was relieved by gracious indifference.

solitary

Too early . . . much too early! I had just dozed off when the padlock clicked and the heavy door grunted open. Now what? I wondered. Can I make it through another day?

Two guards and an officer in pressed uniforms entered the room.

"Today you meet Vietnamese people," the officer directed.

I said nothing, but in my mind flashed scenes of prisoners in bamboo cages being hauled through hamlets.

"You bow head to people," the officer instructed. "I show you right way bow."

Looking away from me, he exacted his regulation bow, which was not just a nod of the head but a full ninety degree bend at the waist. His feet were angled forty-five degrees and the fingers cupped slightly at the seams. The officer stressed the importance of the "correct" procedure and demanded that I render a similar bow. I leaned over, halfheartedly.

"No! This way you must bow," scolded the officer as again he faced away and stooped the full ninety degrees.

Once again I bowed apathetically.

The officer became impatient and shouted at me sternly, but he didn't beat me. I had the feeling that he actually wanted to be accommodating because I was so bruised and swollen and still bleeding at the elbows. I leaned over once more, and this time I met his approval.

One of the guards flung my torn flight suit to the floor, and I was ordered to get dressed. The suit, stripped of its patches, was still wet from the washing it had been given the day before. They unscrewed my handcuffs, and I donned the suit. They did not seem to notice that I had stepped through the cuffs and that my hands were in front of me. If they had noticed, they were probably too embarrassed to admit that I had outmaneuvered them. The guards then dropped a pair of boots next to me. I could tell that they were not mine, especially after I had to force my bare feet into them. They were Gary's—two sizes too small! The guards replaced the cuffs and blindfolded me. I was ready to meet the people.

"You follow orders, I take off cuffs," the officer pledged. I knew better than to make deals with the Vietnamese and would do nothing to embarrass myself or my country.

Dawn. From the Green Knobby Room I was led to another jeep—a cleaner one with no implements to jab me. The perimeter doors clanked, we exited, and after ten or fifteen minutes of travel, the jeep stopped. The guards opened the tailgate and I stumbled out. From the bottom of the blindfold I saw that I was in a rather nice area: a brick tile walkway, trimmed shrubbery, an aluminum and glass door, a terrazzo floor. The officer guided me to a small room and sat me on a wooden chair. From somewhere in the building I could distinguish that a man was delivering a bombastic speech, probably about me; he was interrupted by spasmodic cheers.

The officer briefed me once more: I was to walk with my head down until he gave the command "Let people see face." The guards removed the cuffs, and I pumped my hands and twitched my shoulders to restore circulation. The guards carefully directed me to the door and, removing the blindfold, warned me not to look around. They then prodded me down a hallway, lined with photographers and journalists, a group composed of Orientals and a few Caucasians. With the officer at my side, I walked out of the building onto a patio where a battery of motion picture cameras started whirring. The officer had to shout the command: "Let people see face."

Slowly and deliberately I looked up, stared blankly into space, bowed deeply to the cameras and lowered my head. I was uneasy about this entire charade, feeling a combination of resentment and embarrassment at being featured as a sideshow attraction.

The officer seemed satisfied with the bow and directed me toward the jeep. Two Caucasian photographers approached as if they wanted to say something but didn't dare. For a moment our eyes met. Perhaps they were afraid that I would respond. I have since often wished that I had given them my name and told them to contact my wife, but, as an emergency switch is tied to prevent its being thrown accidentally, I was "safety-wired" to remain mute.

As soon as I was out of the spectators' view, the guards cuffed and blindfolded me. Having accomplished their mission without difficulty they were not so hospitable. The blindfold was cinched so tightly I could see nothing, and the guards became annoyed at my struggle to get back into the jeep. After a ten-minute jostle we arrived at the Hanoi Hilton.

I climbed out of the jeep, but not fast enough to suit the guards. They began pushing and directing me with the points of their bayonets. Of French design, their bayonets would tear the flesh when they were extracted. The guards followed behind me so closely that I became concerned about their careless handling of these weapons. Suddenly the ground gave beneath me! I flinched back to keep from falling. A stinging pain knifed me down into the furrowed *binjo*—an open concrete sewage ditch. My fears were confirmed: A bayonet had ripped my left thigh! I floundered to get up. The guards giggled childishly and cautioned me to keep moving. I limped as hurriedly as I could and was relieved to reach my cell and to sit. The guards removed the manacles and blindfold, made me take off the flight suit, replaced the manacles, and left. I rasped incoherent noises but no one paid any attention. I continued . . . louder now, and finally the officer came.

"You said that if I followed orders, you would take these handcuffs off," I reminded him.

He smiled, shook his head, and left.

I saw a little rag on the floor and after I stepped back through the cuffs, I tried to sop up the blood that was flowing profusely from my thigh. The bayonet had fulfilled the designer's promise. It was a long time before I was convinced that I would not bleed to death. I sat on the concrete floor perplexed about many things. When would the bleeding stop?

What time was it? One . . . maybe two o'clock? I cautiously picked at the dirt in my wounds. Three . . . four o'clock? It seemed to be getting darker. I had never lived through a longer day! Outside my cell I heard the chirping of crickets. It must be seven or eight o'clock. Perhaps I would be allowed to sleep at last.

Just then the officer entered, carrying a sheet of paper. I

noticed immediately that he wore a wristwatch and I focused anxiously on its hands. 10:30? No! It was a trick. It had to be a trick! It was not even midday!

"Here. Read these," the officer said as he handed me the paper. Still anguishing from my discovery of the hour, I stumbled over the copy of poorly written English. Dissatisfied with my clumsy reading, the officer snatched the paper and started reading its contents to me:

You are blackest criminal that this country has ever seen; but due to lenient, humane policy of Vietnamese people, if you follow regulations, you live in peace.

Regulation Number One: Criminals must give full and complete answers to questions asked by Vietnamese guard or officer.

Number Two: Criminals must make no noise in room.

Number Three: Criminals must keep room clean and neat and must not mark in room so graciously given by Vietnamese people.

Number Four: Criminals must get up and go to bed at sound of gong.

Number Five: Criminals must get under bed when imperialist aggressors bomb and strafe our sovereign country.

Number Six: Criminals must say "Bao cao" when they want ask anything.

Number Seven: Criminals must go only in area that guard orders when they go outside of room.

Number Eight: Criminals must bow to every Vietnamese—guards, officers, and people.

Number Nine: Criminals must not bring anything into room from outside.

Number Ten: Criminals must not communicate with or look at other criminals in other room or outside.

With minor variations these were to be the rules for the next six years.

During the following twelve days I was shuffled from room to room. I was moved at least five or six times because the North Vietnamese, having captured more Americans, lacked sufficient cells to house them. To keep me in solitary confinement they moved me from the Green Knobby Room on the third day to what had been a Vietnamese office; it contained only a table and two stools—no bed.

* * *

I still carried ground-in mud from my touchdown, and my wounds—especially at my elbows and thigh—began to fester. When I asked to bathe, the guards told me that I, the imperialist aggressor, had bombed their water supply and that no water was available. But I could see water running freely from an outside faucet. What I did receive was in a chipped porcelain cup, a two-pint container. I had to ration it very carefully and tried to store a little for the end of the day so that I could moisten the rag and sponge my wounds. Generally, due to extreme heat in late May, I had consumed all of it by dusk. I then determined that I must use my urine to wash out the wounds. This measure proved beneficial; at least no serious infection resulted.

On the fourth day the officer handed me a pen and a questionnaire. I completed some questions with the answers I had previously given—my name, place of birth, aircraft, etc. To the other questions, I filled the blanks with lies. I felt uncomfortable about divulging even false information, but it was much wiser to lie than to balk and be beaten beyond rational judgment.

Since the guards had allowed me to complete the questionnaire without their observation, I evasively designed a deck of cards the size of postage stamps on bits of toilet paper. Late at night, with my back to the door, I played solitaire or laid out bridge hands and studied them.

On the fifth day in late morning, I heard a voice outside

my wall. Inspecting each brick, I found a crack big enough to see the lower half of a POW. He was walking back and forth, carrying excrement and bloody bandages to a fenced-in sewage area. I couldn't believe what he was wearing—long pants with alternating gray and red stripes running down the legs! The only thing that the Vietnamese had permitted me to keep were my skivvies, and I thought that this guy was shot down wearing these "northern light long johns" under his flight suit. (It wasn't long before I, too, was issued the same kind of pajamas, and I was proud to spend hours pinching creases into the legs with my thumb and forefinger.)

When the colorful American was inside the sewage enclosure, the guards latched the door and left. About an hour later, after baking in the hot sun, he decided that it was time to utilize the magic phrase from Regulation No. 6—*"Bao cao."* Nothing happened. A little later he uttered another *"Bao cao."* Still nothing. It was noon, and time for siestas. He called a louder "Bao cao." The guards paid no heed. Now the guy, miserably hot and irate, shouted a string of obscenities.

It worked. Guards, familiar with G. I. profanity, swarmed the area to get their fists on him.

Interrogations occurred daily, but officers shifted emphasis from military to political questions. A typical slipshod attempt at brainwashing went something like this:

"You worst criminal. You think you follow international regulations of war?"

"Yes."

"Why? You think United States is doing right?"

"Yes."

"But you know Viet Nam is one country."

"No—North and South."

The interrogator would become riled: "But you are

criminal. You sin. You imperialist aggressor bomb and kill innocent people."

And so the argument would seesaw. If the interrogator ever became tongue-tied or was beaten in the verbal battle, he would leave the room in order to save face. Once a questioner became angry at me and doubled his fist and swung at my face. I jerked back, and his hand ended up in his electric fan, breaking one of its plastic blades. He looked up to see whether I would react, but I knew better. The officer wheeled around and rushed out; I never saw him again. His assistant had to finish the questioning.

During this period of solitary confinement I had much time to think. From the start, I established a definite schedule for personal reflection and appraisal. This included a two-hour worship service in the morning and a similar one in the evening. I spent much time praying—talking informally with God—and recalling as many Scripture verses and Bible stories as I could. I also revived the words and tunes to songs from a Tennessee Ernie Ford album that I'd enjoyed on the *Kitty Hawk*—songs like "Noah," "Peace in the Valley," "Get on Board, Little Children," "Over Jordan." Once in a while, I would start humming too loudly and a guard would bang his rifle against the door. I spent more and more time thinking about intangibles—the purpose for living, ethics, the supernatural, faith, pride—because the tangibles which I had identified with were no longer present—my aircraft, my ship, my personal possessions. This was the onset of thorough reexamination of my life. Often these intricate throught processes ended in slumber.

My cell, an eight-foot square, was in a complex within the Hanoi Hilton that the prisoners named "Little Vegas." Each cell block was named after a casino—"Caesar's Palace," "Thunderbird," "Desert Inn," etc. I spent most of my second week in cell number 7 of the "Stardust." In this cell were four bunks. For a pastime, I assigned to each bunk the name of one of my favorite restaurants: the lower bunks were the "Golden Ox" and the "King's Inn"; the upper, the "Top of the Mark Hopkins" and "Mr. A's." Twice each day when it came time for soup and water, I envisioned the atmosphere of each restaurant and placed the bowl on the bunk which best suited my mood.

I had decided early to devise methods for keeping track of time. I had to be careful not to be obvious about this, however, because the guards were constantly wary of anything that looked like a makeshift device or system. They failed to notice the little grains of sand or bits of straw that I had arranged on a ledge which was once a windowsill. I used the binary system to economize on straws and to reduce chances of disclosure. Even so, I had difficulty telling the date, because the wind would blow the straws away or I'd forget whether I'd added the daily pebble. Within several months, however, any stratagem to tell dates became unnecessary. Instead, the date simply seemed instinctive knowledge. I was able to cross-check my accuracy, though, by the unusually early meal each Sunday.

* * *

Once again the gong sounded its metallic din to another interminable day. Where would I be moved this time? I had last eaten on the upper left bunk, beginning the fifteenth day. So much had happened in two weeks—and yet so little. I sat up and saw that pus still exuded from my wounds. Favoring my left thigh, I returned a straw broom, my makeshift pillow, to its corner. I stunk horribly and daydreamed about showering on the *Kitty Hawk*.

But today was to be different.

Guards opened the latch to the door and, while I was

bowing, entered. With fixed bayonets, they forced me to an area where a heap of ragged clothes—red and gray striped—lay piled on the ground. An officer approached and explained:

"Due to lenient, humane policy of Vietnamese people, we give you imperialist aggressor two pair pant, two shirt, two underpant, two undershirt, one soap, one brush for teeth. Put in net."

I rummaged through the pile looking for what I thought would fit best, and found that each garment was the same size—extra large. I knew that everything was on an "all sales final" basis, but I was afraid to pick through the castoffs too leisurely. The guards did not ascribe to a do-everything-to-please-the-customer policy, so I gathered the least-tattered ones, put them into the net, and was taken back to my room. For hours I inspected my "new" outfits. My excitement mounted as I checked one item at a time. The pants had just a small hole. And the toothbrush—I tried it out, not caring that the dry bristles would make my gums bleed a little. And soap—just like the bars of lye soap Grandma used to make in her big kettle down in the Ozarks.

That evening the guards summoned me to an enclosed, roofless bath area. Inside was a washtub containing cold, dirty water. I stripped and, with my little drinking cup, doused myself with water, lathered with my new bar of soap, and rinsed—shedding a two-week layer of grime and sweat. Then I shaved, using a double-edge razor which had no handle. At last I was "clean"—no itchy beard, no reeking body. I put on my new clothes and wondered what impressions I would now make on the newly captured POWs. Dressed in fresh habiliment, I experienced a sublime physical and mental catharsis. Even the pain of my wounds seemed to wash away with the filth.

Fifteen minutes later I was back in my cell, reinspired to

outlast any Vietnamese endeavor to debase me. The door opened. I waited for something to happen. And then, in the doorway sauntered a tall man, back hunched and forehead deeply lined. He studied me with uncertain eyes.

An American—another American! I rushed to the door as quickly as I could and grasped his hand—a hand which was completely numb from inadequate circulation at the elbows.

"Hi," I said, "I'm Charlie Plumb."

routine

During my six years' imprisonment, countless incidents and adjustments occurred—the changing North Vietnamese political and military complexion which resulted in a tightening or relaxing of restrictions, new cellmates, increased sophistication of our clandestine communications network, etc. The size of our cells and the number of men in them also offered particular problems and necessitated adjustments.

Altogether, I made eight moves to different camps, and the number of cellmates ranged from one to fifty-six.

Date	No. Cellmates	Camp
3 June 67	1	Hanoi Hilton (Hoa Lo) and Plantation
29 Oct 67	2	Plantation and Zoo
30 July 69	3	Zoo
30 Sep 70	7	Camp Faith (Third Base)

Date	No. Cellmates	Camp
24 Nov 70	56 to 35	Hanoi Hilton
11 Nov 71	3	Zoo and Hanoi Hilton
14 May 72	7 to 1	Dogpatch
20 Jan 73	19	Hanoi Hilton

In many respects, the number of cellmates had little effect on my personal life-style. Communicating from a small room to the other POWs was more difficult and time-consuming than in the larger rooms, but it took place nevertheless. And whether I was with two men or with fifty-six, my daily chores changed little.

By 1969 a somewhat "normal" pattern of everyday living gradually developed. Adherence to this schedule helped us promote unity and acquire the physical and mental health necessary to endure our adversities.

At the 6:30 a.m. gong most of the prisoners devoted a half hour to prayer and/or meditation. After the customary "Good morning," the cell became quiet. I assiduously placed sketches of Anne on my bunk and reminisced about the many good times we had had together. I daily resolved to become an exemplary husband for her and father for our future children; and I was determined that these lessons in patience, self-sacrifice, discipline, humility, and pride of achievement would one day accompany me back home.

At 7:00 a.m. I put the sketches back into my cup lid and practiced my "piano." A lover of music, I had always wanted to be able to play but had never taken lessons. I knew, though, that my hand could span nine notes on a keyboard; thus I scratched out three octaves of black and white keys on one of the bunk boards. I practiced the scales going up with one hand and down with the other. Then I practiced chords. I didn't make much music, but I didn't make much noise either. After several years of these "lessons" I reached a point where I could actually hear the notes in my mind. I kept my hands busy and my attention fully committed—and another hour passed.

At 8:00 we did exercises—push-ups, leg-lifts, sit-ups, pressing bunk boards, and infinite improvisations to augment stamina and muscle tone. Initially, the guards were furious when they saw us running in place, the perspiration running down our bodies, and they pounded on the door and screamed. We immediately had to take our places and offer the deep bow. After we were certain they had left, we resumed the exercises. As the years progressed, the guards exhibited less concern; consequently, we were able to sustain up to an hour and a half of exercise with only two or three interrupting bows.

Our imaginary school bell rang at 9:30. Time for academics. Although most of us were college graduates, firsthand experience and formal instruction at the high school level were the bases for our curricula. Of course we had no teaching aids—no pencils, paper, chalkboards, or books, but no one could imprison our minds and our thoughts. (Often in my dreams, I must admit, I envisioned leaving the Hanoi Hilton, going home, looking for and finding a brand-new yellow pencil, and bringing it back to my cell. Or I would dream of entering shops containing nothing but rows and rows of pencils. I've never since taken a pencil for granted.)

The synapse of our nervous systems opened wide to give and receive any fragments of knowledge we could share. Foreign languages, biology, history, and geography were standard subjects. Mathematics, geometry, algebra, and trigonometry were favorites because they required the most time. We must have derived every existing Euclidian formula.

Geography was another popular course; each tutor described his native state and hometown, giving as many particulars as he could recall. Several of the fellows had lived in foreign countries, were fluent in the language, and they spent countless hours teaching verb lists and conjugations. By the time we were released, many of us had grasped a smattering of French, Spanish, Russian, and German. The important thing at the time was that the tempo of the bland hours was accelerated.

The academics were not limited to the men in a particular cell. Information passed through the channels of our secret network so that a row of cells in a block more closely resembled an open forum than confinement. Obviously, we had problems—trying to relay a geometric symbol or a German umlaut. And at times the information was misunderstood and its validity questionable. But we learned it anyway—just to pass the time. "Last-minute" cramming was never one of our problems, but it was common to hear: "I've got to get these genders straightened out before I have to go home."

The longer we were in prison, the more accurate and refined the subject matter became. For example, when I first "hooked into" the communications net, I took a biology course, three hours in duration. Six years later I "enrolled" in the course again under the same instructor, Joe Milligan. Through a process of heavy concentration and cross-reference with other POWs, Joe taught the course for six months, five hours a week. He had us memorizing the Latin taxonomy from protozoa to mammalia.

One of the courses I taught was photography, which lasted one hour a day for a month. I included all the fundamentals of the subject: the physics of light, the chemistry involved in developing and printing, the geometry of composition. I also assigned a "show and tell," and my students depicted imaginary pictures they had snapped with imaginary cameras.

Finally, at 10:30, chow time! We could hear that it was forthcoming when the guards quit playing volleyball, when the chopping of cleavers ceased, or when a chogey pole (a split bamboo pole used by the guards to carry soup kettles) clattered outside our door. Twenty hours had passed since the last "soft diet," and like Pavlov's dogs, we began to salivate. Any prisoner close enough to the kitchen to smell or to see what was on the menu would tap out the news on the net. He didn't need a French dictionary: "C" meant cabbage soup; "T" turnip soup; "P" for Plumb's favorite—pumpkin soup.

Our approach to the soup was, "If this is coffee, give me tea. If this is tea, give me coffee." And if it had been poured through an empty strainer the strainer would have remained nearly empty. Occasionally such condiments as an onion or a piece of garlic would rest, like a single marble, at the bottom of the kettle. The soup was even more insulting, served with spoons hammered from shot-down American aircraft.

Either rice or stale bread attended the cuisine. But to have this quasi-solid food was no cause to rejoice. The rice was used to camouflage insidious little worms; especially during the summer each spoonful was seasoned with at least a dozen of them. The first few times after we discerned the soft pupae we tried to alienate them from the rice grains, but it was too tedious, and the eating period was over before our chow was half-finished. Complaints were to no avail; the V officers said they ate them, too. Rice was easier to eat when we closed our eyes, but we couldn't turn off our imaginations.

The bread contained weevils—the hard-shelled, crunchy

type—and little rocks. To save our teeth, we soon learned to perform the old soft chew, spitting out the slag.

"Meat" was a rare treat. Little triangles of barely cooked pork, like a plug from a watermelon, occasionally floated in the murky soup. On the apex of the plug was a meager tittle of flesh—maybe—below that lard, then the rind and red skin with its bristles and hairs. Flotsam in a polluted pond! This grotesque hunk of hog, often rotten, was cooked right along with the soup, so its removal failed to warm many appetites. Neither did the V's assurance that trichinosis was peculiar to American hogs.

Within a couple of months our starving bodies superseded our sensitivity. We certainly needed protein, and the lard might help fill the gaps between our ribs. After six months—what the heck?—down the hatch went pig bristles and all.

On special occasions, we would have a side plate of salty fish heads or granulated Cuban sugar. The punsters regarded our request for stewed bananas as "fruitless."

That we had to bow deeply to every approaching North Vietnamese became an increasingly grim exercise, especially for the older fellows. Each time the guards opened the hinged flap on the cell door we had to rush to our respective spots on the floor. They incessantly peeked into the rooms trying to catch us at some wrongdoing. This perpetual invasion of privacy and its accompanying humiliation so unnerved us at times that we found it more agonizing than physical torture. Night or day, if a guard wanted to play this game of torment, he peeked in ten or twenty times in fifteen minutes, and each time we had to jump to attention and bow. Normally, we were bothered only about once each hour at irregular intervals—except for siesta.

From 11:30 a.m. to 2:00 p.m., the guards apparently

took naps and the chances of espial lessened. But for the Americans, it was time for communications. We came out of the woodwork—or rather the woodwork became a part of us as we tapped on the walls, pulled wires, coughed or wheezed our coded messages. The information being passed from room to room was generally mundane—Mom's recipe for chocolate pie, a sister's measurements, our plans in Vegas when we got out. Classified information was rarely put on the "comm net."

Siesta over, the chogey poles again clattered and our mouths watered. This meal, same as the first. I remember one hundred consecutive meals of the same soup. Good thing it was my favorite—pumpkin!

At 2:30 "academics" began again. Frequently the lessons were interrupted by V officers taking a student away from "class" to dispense a little of their own "political science." At bayonet point, another feeble attempt at brainwashing was undertaken by the naïve officers who were confident that their personal techniques could break our will. The interrogations went something like this:

"Why you criminals come to Viet Nam, an innocent country?"

We would look askance with a provoked stare.

The determined officer continued his inane questioning until his list was exhausted. And the spaces left for writing in answers remained blank.

Dusk was "show time." The fellows took turns narrating movies they had seen before they were "killed" (shot down). Scene by scene, the POW performed his histrionics until the plot was so complex and confused that a denouement was impossible. A description of the heroine was an especial challenge—her low-cut gown, her seductive smile, her inevitable trip to the bedroom. I had to quit listening to them because they hurt more than they entertained. "Low-cost" productions, lasting about fifteen minutes in 1967, became full-blown spectaculars six years later. The same film blossomed to a three-hour epic, with no intermission. And it collapsed from a rating of "PG" to "XXX."

We established all kinds of contests to relieve the tedium. The crazier the competition the better! Having no materials, we had to rely on our ingenuity.

As one example, we devised a "low and slow" contest to herald pilots who had been bagged at the most crucial low altitude and slow airspeed. The contest was won by a dark horse, Seaman Doug Hegdahl, who was washed ashore after falling off a cruiser—twenty-three feet at sixteen knots!

Toward nightfall a guard often brought to the smokers their Vietnamese cigarettes—three a day in 1967, six a day in late 1969. All of us would have to face the door and bow, and then the smokers would extend their hands. Invariably, the guard dropped the cigarettes to the floor and laughed as the humbled smoker leaned down to pick them up. Once the smoker had his cigarettes, he could only look at them until the guard brought by a smoldering punk at chow the next morning. The smoker would have to decide whether to eat after his twenty-one-hour fast or chainsmoke his three "weeds."

Eventually, the smokers learned to make their own punks by rationing toilet paper and rolling it into long strands. Some of the punks were thirty or forty feet long, coiled like a skein of yarn. Once lit, they would burn all day if unraveled every ten minutes or so. The punk was forgotten one day, and the entire coil ignited, sending little glows up the paper threads in all directions. Smoke filtered through the air, bringing stern warnings from the nonsmokers who had already contributed their share of toilet paper. They didn't relish the thought of having to walk around with their left hands behind their backs.

Another problem arose whenever a nonsmoker gave his cigarettes away, only to see the smoker, now with a surplus, trade cigarettes for someone else's piece of bread or banana. But, like other problems, this was resolved. And the toilet paper kept smoldering.

At dark, the prison camp often suffered a power failure. Guards did not dare enter our pitch-black cells, so we could get by with actions that were normally prohibited. In the small or large rooms someone would start singing one of his favorite hymns or songs, and soon the entire group would join in. We could hear the guards banging and warning us to cease, but we knew that they would not brave darkness to do anything about it. It was great to join together and harmonize.

Mine eyes have seen the glory of the coming of the Lord.
He is trampling out the vintage where the grapes of wrath are stored.
He hath loosed the fateful lightning of his terrible swift sword.
His truth is marching on.
Glory, glory, hallelujah!

vietnamese pastimes

From the very beginning of my imprisonment I made every effort to size up my captors, closely observing them and evaluating their behavior. I was often wrong in my early assessments, but supplemental lumps on my head soon made me more perceptive. Anxieties toward them therefore diminished as my shrewdness increased.

Most of the input was, of course, covert. A crack in a brick or a hole gnawed by rats in the wall became my visual passport to this foreign land. Even though my vision and scope were limited, my observations over an extended period of time were probably more accurate than those of foreign visitors who saw only Vietnamese propaganda.

Once I constructed a mirror by daily polishing a small piece of mahogany with earwax. I fastened this improvisation to the upper side of a ventilation hole and saw reversed images of an already topsy-turvy situation. Often I would devote three to four hours daily to peephole reconnaissance.

What I saw was a kaleidoscope of the mundane, the tragic, the humorous, the paradoxical—a conglomerate of human emotion and response. Nevertheless, any individual standards of behavior in the North Vietnamese populace were predicated on an almost inherent acceptance of the doctrine and control by the state. Consistent with this attitude, separation of militia and peasant was not significant: the Vietnamese considered themselves as essential members of the "People's Army" whose duty it was to vanquish every "bellicose warmonger" and "perfidious aggressor."

It was therefore not surprising that the V military personnel rarely wore uniforms or special attire to distinguish themselves from the civilian. Soldiers, like the peasants, felt as though they were locked together in the same closet of U.S. oppression; and this viewpoint was constantly reinforced by government propaganda. Thus, no clear chain of command appeared in the lower echelons. Even Catholicism underwent an ironic metamorphosis: Christ himself was epitomized as the typical socialist peasant who, born in a lowly condition, labored and sacrificed in order to win the ultimate victory over intruding evil.

The North Vietnamese frequently seemed childish and immature. For example, early one morning I peeked through a nail hole in my cell door and saw two guards approaching a jeep which had been junked in the open center of our camp. It was still intact but lacked a running gear. While the guards walked around it, their conversation became louder than usual. One of the men decided to go for a ride in the "lame duck" and hopped into the driver's seat, followed by the second guard on the other side. The driver pretended to put a key into the ignition and then hit the starter button on the floor. As he did, he made engine noises with his mouth. He pumped on the throttle and accelerated his vocal chords. By this time, the other man was ready to go. The driver pushed the clutch, put the transmission in gear, and grunted an original gutteral backfire. They were off!

The driver jostled up and down as though he were driving the jeep along a bumpy road and steering to avoid what must have been especially heavy pedestrian traffic. The fellow riding "shotgun" suddenly realized that he was on the same road and started swaying in rhythm with the driver, adding to the horsepower with his own mouth. Bumping down the street, they turned and twisted each switch, knob, and gauge. Completing the "checklist" they once again manipulated every panel button. After half an hour, their interest spent, these "distinguished wardens of enemy captives" climbed out and, arm in arm, walked away kicking at rocks.

The frequent manner in which grown men primped furnished more evidence of adolescent behavior. At first I was startled to see guards stop to admire themselves in the window glass of an empty room. Smiling, talking, and even singing to their personified egos, they combed and recombed their coal-black hair and repicked their pimpled faces. They never missed an opportunity to preen.

This ego extended to "private" possessions as well. Whenever a Vietnamese claimed a pen, pocketknife, or wristwatch as his own (not the state's), he perpetually showed it to anyone he thought was watching. If he had a watch he'd raise his arm ostentatiously every two minutes to check the time.

The contents of a Vietnamese billfold were far more confidential. Prisoners of war never warranted the "honor" of being shown these items as fellow Vietnamese often were. Our "perusal" was limited to cursory glances through cracks, and we could see that the billfolds contained pictures of girl friends or wives and children and personal letters. They rarely

contained money, but even so it would have bought very little.

Although one's personal possessions were exciting status symbols, the property of another was not. Each Vietnamese had to keep his "valuables" under constant lock and key to prevent their disappearing. Such measures were frequently futile. I once saw a guard carry another soldier's locked bicycle to a tree and use it as a makeshift ladder so that he could poke at a bird's nest with his stick. The bicycle's fenders were soon bent and the spokes broken. The guard was able to knock down the nest, however, and to him that was all that mattered.

Except for propaganda equipment, the possessions of the state were not held sacrosanct either. No item, regardless of its obvious worth, escaped the possibility of being misused. All that was necessary was that the item be nearby at the time it was needed.

A typical incident occurred later in my internment. The Vietnamese officers had presented my cellmates and me a deck of Eastern European playing cards. For us these were priceless, because they represented hours of relief from boredom. We were fastidious about caring for the deck, stacking them in piles to eliminate shuffling and mindfully wiping all cards after we finished using them. One day, while we were playing bridge, five or six guards outside our building started beating at tree branches with bamboo poles in order to scare out a bird. We welcomed the startled denizen as it flew through the vent of "Barn 4," our fourteen-by-fourteen-foot cell. Like Cub Scouts spotting a rabbit, the soldiers shouted in frenzied Vietnamese that the bird had found refuge in our cell.

They charged Barn 4, groping for the right key to open our door. Once inside the cell they flailed and swatted recklessly until they knocked the bird to the floor. Injured, it crawled under one of our bunks and into a crack so small that a guard could only poke at it with his fingertips. Frustrated, he looked around for something to pry it out.

Unfortunately, on the bunk lay the deck of cards. Immediately he grabbed a card and slid under the bunk. We riveted our eyes to the floor and grimaced. After much scraping, the guard crawled out holding the mutilated card—ruined for no reason! The small-game hunters departed empty-handed. Hours later, the bird ventured out. We tried to nurse it back to health, but it was too abused to save. So was our six of spades.

Vietnamese sadism was often directed toward wildlife. Soldiers would catch a baby bird just learning to fly and pull the feathers out of one wing. Released, it would become an easy target for rock-throwing.

Animals which the V slaughtered for eating often suffered a similar painful demise. I've seen many holiday chickens and turkeys meet their Waterloo after thirty or forty minutes of failing to dodge stones or sticks. Even then, rather than being killed instantly, they were generally punctured in an artery or vein and left to bleed to death.

Probably the most sadistic practice of all was a game involving mice or puppies. Guards would douse them with gasoline, set them on fire, and turn them loose to squeal and scurry in search of relief from the heat. Then the soldiers would chase them with sticks, playing polo with their live fireballs until the little animals blackened and died.

* * *

We respected those Vietnamese guards who performed their duties toward us in a responsible military manner. There were some occasions, however, when V soldiers delighted in cruelty for cruelty's sake. No rationalization was necessary for these embittered individuals to regard us as something less than small animals. They descended below the atrocities of battle and mocked war itself. One guard—we called him "Afterbirth"—was incredibly sadistic. Even the Vietnamese officers could not control him. Crazed by hatred, he defiantly stole from us, harassed and tortured us, and framed us in an effort to destroy our unity. Would that "Afterbirth" had never been born! But he was. Most of the Vietnamese were of a less violent nature, subsisting as best they could under war's *Sturm und Drang*.

Still, the V didn't have to be sick to avoid work. I witnessed hours of carefree laziness, particularly in the Vietnamese men. In Viet Nam, women's liberation is a fact of life, and the men gladly accept it. They don't boss the women around; instead, they permit them to do 90 percent of the work—and not necessarily because of the shortage of manpower during wartime. On numerous occasions I have seen males squatting around the lip of a deep hole smoking cigarettes and whittling sticks while young girls tossed mud and dirt with small entrenching tools to the ground level above. I have seen petite women carry as much as two hundred pounds on their chogey poles and overtake meandering males on the way to market.

Incidentally, three- and four-year-old youngsters were given bamboo poles to learn how to carry supplies. The method required balance, strength, and rhythm. A chogey pole was placed on one shoulder, and loaded wicker baskets—sometimes three and four feet in diameter—were hung from each end. Then the bandy-legged peasant would walk quickly with one hand on the pole and the other hanging away from the body as a counterbalance. Frequently callouses and open sores formed on the shoulders; but at the same time, carriers developed amazing back and shoulder

muscles. With heavy, awkward poles, women wobbled through narrow doors and up and down stairways. American POWs, larger and stronger, could not duplicate the balance and timing and could be outperformed by young girls.

The women not only were the principal workers but assumed the aggressive role in the battle between the sexes, teasing and chasing males who often appeared completely indifferent. Perhaps the wartime ratio of men to women was so favorable to available males that they could play hard to get. In any case, the men seemed to have little use for female flirtation. They did, however, display an especial affection toward their male comrades. On rare occasion, guards even propositioned POWs, but they never pressed the issue. As a matter of fact, most of the guards were embarrassed to see an undressed American sitting on the "honey bucket," and they made every effort to keep us from seeing them unclothed.

Even so, these men had no qualms about sexual exposure to each other. It was common to see two V guards or officers holding hands, walking arm in arm, reaching hands under one another's clothing, or lying in the undergrowth with their bodies intertwined. Of course they exhibited this conduct without the awareness that we could see them.

One miserably hot afternoon in the summer of 1967 my conversation with Kay was disrupted by a lilting song originating from outside our cell wall. The voice was tender and beautiful. I knew that a bath area was only a short distance from our wall and, not having seen a female for a long time, I sprang to the window. My hopes were encouraged as a sweet fragrance drifted into our stale cell. Although the crack in the wood was at such a poor angle I could not see the bath area well, I peeped anyway. A pair of dainty feet stepped into view.

"Hey!" I whispered to my mate. "Come here!"

Both of us glued our eyes to cracks, muttering a "Come on!" to ourselves as the feet moved back and forth. A small, shapely hand placed a pink bar of scented soap on the ledge. "Come on! Come on!"

We gasped. It was too much. I thought of those teasing knee-on-down camera angles of a 1960 movie—and in color. Bright-red bikini panties fell to her feet!

The siren song continued. We breathed harder. "Closer! Closer!"

She came closer. Her knees, her thighs, her . . . her . . .

His! . . . how utterly disgusting!

Yes, there he was, a Vietnamese soldier, waltzing around with nothing on but perfume.

vietnamese behavior

I was impressed with the apparent high morality between male and female. Although I perceived nearly all of the women as most unattractive, I'm sure this was not the cause for their puritanical ethics. The males simply never seemed to be "on the prowl." I saw nothing suggestive or permissive—no petting or pinching. That is, not between men and women.

The Vietnamese told us via propaganda broadcasts that extramarital sex and prostitution were unlawful; and having many opportunities to peer into the city streets, I cannot disprove that information. Houses of prostitution probably do exist, but they certainly were not obvious.

One of the frequent arguments used against POWs during interrogations was the statement that American soldiers had debased the South Vietnamese society. Often officers showed us pictures of bars and brothels in Saigon, and after using these accusatory exhibits, sermonized about how morally upstanding the Vietnamese were in the North. I knew that V propaganda was exaggerated, but if anything contained a grain of truth, it was the charge concerning American moral indecency in South Viet Nam.

On one occasion, we discovered that a copy of *Playboy* magazine had been sent from the States to POWs. Of course, no one in our group was ever permitted to look through it, but the officers and guards did. Outwardly they showed dismay, but they were noticeably enticed—like little kids sneaking behind the barn to look at "dirty" pictures.

Excluding heterosexual morality, the Vietnamese should receive low marks in behavior. Stealing someone's possessions (at least, what he claimed to be his) didn't seem to bother anyone except the "owner." An extensive black market thrived from the sale of stolen goods. Many items designated for POWs were pilfered by guards and sold in alleyways. For example, razor blades issued to POWs would often disappear; guards, who shaved rarely if at all, would pawn them for food or money.

Punishment for stealing was token. Once an officer caught a guard stealing a POW handkerchief issued to us near the time of our release. The only apparent disciplinary action taken against him was the withholding of his cigarette ration for several days.

Lying was also a Vietnamese way of life. Deception was rampant—both up and down the chain of command. A guard would steal one of our meals and report to his officer that we'd had the usual two servings. To his superior, the officer stretched the lie to two *good* meals. The superior officer reported to his general that we had eaten *three* good meals. No one asked us why we were so hungry.

Guards resorted to stealing our food because they, too, were hungry. North Viet Nam is a poor country where surplus food has never been a problem. The people did eat more meat than was given us, however, and they generally drank sweetened tea or a fruit punch during work breaks.

As food selection was simple, so too was its preparation. Even though guards had their own mess hall, they abandoned it at least five or six times a week to prepare their own meals. To do this, they gathered wood and started a fire, often so close to the prison wall that smoke poured into our cells. Then they placed a pot of water on the fire, waited for it to boil, and tossed in their culinary mainstay—weeds. Forced to eat weeds entirely too often, I could never imagine what horrible concoction was being prepared in the kitchen to make the guards desert it.

On special holidays, such as Tet, the V would throw in a goose or puppy as a special ingredient. Guards used a kitchen cleaver to cut the goose at the neck, and a cup to catch the blood. They hammered on the fowl in order to fragment the bones inside, after which they plucked the feathers. When the water was hot, they dipped the goose into the pot and pulled it out to pick pinfeathers. Once more they dashed the cleaver against the flesh, further splintering the bones. At last, the goose was sliced into several pieces and boiled. Although the meat was difficult to eat (we were occasionally served meat prepared in this manner), the guards informed us that the bone marrow made it more nutritious. I suppose they were correct, but it was hard on gums.

Besides their two meals a day, workmen took a break once in the morning. Each man brought along a net which contained, among other things, a little china tea set. At break time he rummaged through the net, located his demitasse cup, and poured in a swallow or two of sweetened tea. At times he chomped on a stalk of sugar cane. During their break, workers talked and laughed, drank their tea, and smoked. Men often "rolled their own" and puffed effeminately, holding the cigarettes between their thumb and forefinger and extending their "pinkie." Most of the smokers had tobacco stains and burn scars on their lips (as did many POW smokers).

After break the workers placed their cups in the nets until siesta. At approximately 11:00 a.m. the nets would again be opened, the daily articles removed, and the nets tied to elm or oak trees to form hammocks. Laborers always took advantage of siesta, often oversleeping and straggling back to work late. Some would go to the well to wash their faces, and some seemed satisfied not to reawaken at all. They generally sat around most of the day anyway, so the siesta granted little break in the monotony.

Maintaining current wardrobes was never a problem for the Vietnamese. Fashions remained the same. Men wore khaki shirts and pants with legs cut off above the knees if they had to slog in the rice paddies. Women wore the same kind of shirts and black baggy pants. On Sunday afternoons, the women exchanged their work shirts for high-collared white blouses, but the pants were the same. Seldom did I see makeup or jewelry. From strings of laundry hanging down the walls of the camp, I was able to determine that the women still hadn't adopted the no-bra look—although I couldn't see why bras were needed. In fact, many women wore falsies.

All of the people attired themselves with conical straw hats for protection against the sun and rain. Often the hats were removed and used as fans, and I could see that pictures of Ho Chi Minh or the national flag or a girl were glued inside.

The strangest accouterments, winning hands down, were the belts. Some country must have unloaded a million of them on the North Vietnamese. It would not have been so bad except that each buckle was monogrammed. Guards, some ten or fifteen of them, traipsed by our cell throughout the day, and every one of them featured the same letter on his buckle: "C." The next morning, the fad changed: "L." The guards didn't mind; they had no awareness of fashion whatsoever. They didn't even seem to care that the belts were much too long for their narrow waists and had to be wrapped all the way to the back.

Although the intention was not to spearhead latest trends in fashion, there was one effort which unequivocally affected some of the women's appearance. I suspect that a leading "medical authority" had announced his discovery of a surefire means to prevent tooth decay. What was it? Lacquer. Black lacquer. Permanent black lacquer.

Not to help the matter, the Vietnamese women also loved to chew tobacco. It, too, served a medicinal function— deadening the nerves of rotting teeth. The dilemma faced by the women was that the tobacco, while relieving pain, also contributed further to the decay. Available space for a pouch depended on the number of remaining teeth.

Nicotine was not the only drug in common use. Especially on Sunday afternoons I saw natives strive for and reach their "highs" on opium.

Opium was cheap and available. (Use of the more expensive alcohol, therefore, was quite uncommon, although officers did occasionally drink wine or beer.) Glassy-eyed guards frequently used opium to erase any sensitivity while torturing POWs.

Personal hygiene was not important to the Vietnamese. Although the city people generally smelled less offensive than the country peasants, they all reeked. Obviously, some of the people put too much faith in their perfumes.

To make sure that POWs were abiding by camp regulations, Rule Number Three (Criminals must keep room clean and neat . . .), the prison medic came into our cells about once a week for inspection. Each time he entered, we were required to hold our hands high above our heads while he thoroughly frisked us and rummaged through every item in the room. Our clothing, folded with painstaking care, was searched and strewn to the floor. Precious bars of soap were probed by pocketknives and broken. Efforts to find contraband were an obsession with the guards, with a surprising exception—areas above the inspector's eye level received little more than a quick glance.

One morning the medic lifted a rice mat (our sleeping mat) on the top bunk and found dust. Through his interpreter he inveighed: "Room filthy. You get sick from filthy room. If not clean next time, you will be punish!"

He glanced up. In the corner of the ceiling were cobwebs. Furious, he pointed up and screamed: "Room filthy! Filthy! You clean now!"

We had nothing to use for cleaning—unless we threw our shirts high into the corner.

With that the medic turned to leave. Before he did, though, he hacked up a big "goober" and deposited it on our floor. We were stunned. There it was, coming from the one man we had to rely on for medical treatment. And moments earlier, this same man had displayed fury because of a little dust. Did he do it for spite? Or would he have spat in his own house? I don't know, but we were careful where we stepped the rest of the day.

In the summer our cells were so foul smelling that the V inspection team refused to enter until guards had opened the doors for several minutes to allow the air to freshen.

Other than common family remedies of weeds and roots, medication for the people was not readily available. The state promoted health but had few facilities and pharmaceuticals for the ill.

Physical fitness programs were broadcast throughout the cities and hamlets via propaganda facilities. Shortly after I was imprisoned I was awakened by an announcer's rhythmic cant to march: "Mot, hai, ba, bon; Mot, hai, ba, bon" (One, two, three, four). Although radios occasionally blared all night, this particular morning's sign-on was at 5:00 a.m.

I thought, These people are really industrious . . . getting up this early for exercises. I went to a crack in the door to see what was happening.

Nothing was happening. The march music continued, as did the counting. Some North Vietnamese Jack LaLanne was vocalizing his physical fitness program. From that morning to the time of my release, I saw no more than two or three people get up and drag halfheartedly through the motions.

The majority of the people did manual labor and ate very few rich foods, so they had no problem with obesity. On their own time, and probably for enjoyment rather than therapy, they did ritualistic Oriental dances which resembled a combination of stylized boxing jabs and a cheerleader's routine. But they didn't get up with the chickens to do it.

Interest in stylistic, precise movements seemed to carry over into the classroom. Children apparently practiced hour after hour to perfect a beautiful, delicate script. Often we were ridiculed for our sloppy handwriting.

Artwork was also stressed in the child's education. Graffiti, designed from a child's fantasy, reflected the state's educational curricula. Most of the creations were political or military in nature: a dove, or an American aircraft being shot down by Vietnamese artillery, or a child carrying a banner. They used pieces of brick for chalk, and sides of buildings— sometimes freshly painted—for chalkboards. Property of the state was fair game for individual expression—as long as the artwork was "properly" expressed.

Reading material was abundant. North Vietnamese often walked around with books bulging in their pockets. Without exception, the subject matter was political, usually Russian. The *Communist Manifesto,* writings of Marx, Engels, Lenin (I saw none by Chairman Mao) constituted the bulk of the material. Perhaps these books were the only ones available, or perhaps they were the only ones to pass censorship. In any case, the soldiers and the people in general were literate and seemed to enjoy reading.

Not once did I see any printed matter—a book, magazine, newspaper, lyrics to songs, written speeches, or billboards—that contained anything but propaganda. I was given the understanding that writers, artists, and journalists were required to take a solemn oath to promote in every work the "people's fight against obdurate aggression and world hegemony."

The Vietnamese seemed to understand the fundamental theories of mathematics, algebra, and trigonometry, but they didn't have the material resources to apply this knowledge practically. Nor were they able to express their knowledge succinctly, especially during philosophical arguments. The Vietnamese language lacks "sophisticated" words which describe abstract concepts, and entire paragraphs are needed to express a thought which can be conveyed with three or four words of English. A Vietnamese word root is often loaded with parasitic prefixes and suffixes in an attempt to enhance meaning.

During my imprisonment, the North Vietnamese landed another "first" in the history of their country. They published a dictionary of their native language. Until that time their primary dictionary was a "pointie-talkie,"* compliments of downed Navy and Air Force pilots.

Once when I saw the V propaganda newspaper (published in English and designed to raise doubts or break spirits) I immediately noticed a large headline on the front page: "World Famous Agronomist Revolutionizes Rice Planting Technique." I visualized mammoth machinery pushing through the mud without getting stuck while peasants stood alongside the embankment in wonderment. I read on. The article began with a listing of the discoverer's academic qualifications. This fellow had doubtlessly taken every botany course in the Orient. Then followed a lengthy discussion about the happiness and pride he felt while serving his struggling country and helping it overcome the oppression of the fascist-capitalist warmongers. The essence of the article was summed up in a brief paragraph.

For 4,000 years the Vietnamese people have been laboring, sweating, and toiling in the mud and water of rice paddies. We have discovered a revolutionary method of planting rice. Through extensive research we have found that, instead of grasping the rice sprouts and planting them with the palm of the hand facing downward, it is much more efficient to plant the rice sprouts with the palm of the hand facing upward.

After four thousand years of doing it wrong, peasants throughout the country are now using this revolutionary new approach to planting—and North Vietnamese technology is on the move.

The propaganda newspapers given us were consistently ludicrous. Many of us read them just to pass the time and to search for any hint of current events which might be extracted from the gobbledegook. The manner in which we

---

*A "pointie-talkie" is a phrase dictionary of many languages carried by pilots so that they can communicate with the local population.

learned about the American moon shot is typical. We first became acquainted with our space success in the winter of 1969 from a Vietnamese news release:

Russians have beaten the Americans in the great space race. They have won sure and certain technological victories over the United States because they have successfully landed a lunar vehicle to explore the entire surface of the moon and to gather its samples. Unlike the inferior American space effort, the Russians did not have to send a man along to control the vehicle. Instead, they used the latest automatic signaling devices, instructing the vehicle to do whatever they wished. Unquestionably, the USSR has advanced years ahead of the lagging American space effort.

The official news releases submitted for dissemination were rarely if ever challenged by the North Vietnamese population. Gullible peasants and soldiers alike simply believed what they read or were told. After I had been in prison for about six months and had been subjected to hundreds of interrogations, I was becoming extremely weary of the same mundane questions put to me at each session. Once a young Vietnamese officer, fresh out of language school, showed up as my interrogator. He had never spoken to an American before and was dumbfounded at my responses to his stale questions. In broken English, he pietistically deduced: "You here six whole month. You still not see truth! How is possible?"

I'd had plenty of time—much more than was necessary—to see that his "truth" was nothing more than a fool's tale. No person with the slightest discernment could possibly miss the fallacies in the propaganda. Yet, it happened all the time. Like this novice, the Vietnamese expressed amazement when I did not agree that their black was white.

Knowing when to disagree openly with the questioner or guard and when to remain silent was often difficult. We were subjected to beatings either way. We did learn, however, that we must not assume too much. Guards were never "English-speakers"; they were not allowed to learn English . . . or so we thought. In the winter of 1967, we were recipients of a series of embittered cruelties from an especially mean guard we called Fubar. Angry POWs muttered choice epithets under their breaths within earshot of Fubar whenever the occasion called for it—which was often. No matter how horrible the insult, he never flinched.

It was Christmas, and I was feeling especially nostalgic when suddenly our door opened and the terrible guard entered and said: "Molly Cleemas. You zrink coffay?"

My mouth dropped. After all these months and all our derision, Fubar revealed his heretofore hidden knowledge of English. It was frightening. We recalled too easily what we had last said to him. Was revenge going to be his "Cleemas" present?

For six months this guard had not said a word of English or even slightly reacted to our diatribes. Characteristic of the Vietnamese manner of saving face, this "Francis the Talking Mule" was not affronted by our abuse until he thought we knew that he understood. I can still picture it: "Molly Cleemas. You zrink coffay?" We did drink the coffee, and we swallowed hard.

vietnamese culture

At many of the interrogations, the officers exposed a real curiosity toward America's consumer products: air conditioning, electrical appliances, speedboats, automobiles, airplanes. To them, it was completely inconceivable that one person could, by himself, own these things—a notion comparable, I suppose, to our thinking that a person could own his own spaceship. In Viet Nam a boat or an airplane is something that only the state can afford.

Driving a car simply for pleasure was a circumstance which also boggled their minds. Vehicles were known by them to have only strict utilitarian function, chiefly military. During one interrogation, the officer asked me about the things I owned. I described my car and explained that we could travel seventy or eighty miles per hour from one city to another—and even one hundred miles per hour if we had to. As usual, he refused to recognize U.S. technological superiority by rationalizing it away with "Ah yes. In North

Viet Nam, however, we have much better approach. You notice we build curvy roads with many holes. We want our people go slow so they not kill themselves." Then he asked, "What good is car?"

I answered, "It takes me from one place to another."

"But can you put pigs in it?"

"No."

"Coal?"

"No."

"Firewood?"

"No."

"What do you carry in it? Market vegetables?"

"Just myself."

He walked out of the room, convinced that I was telling more lies.

He *knew* these were lies because, like other information, my answers didn't jibe with official North Vietnamese propaganda. For example, according to official "facts" only the upper class could use the U.S. roadways. None of the American "peasants" had access to them. The Vietnamese officers believed that fully one-third of the American population was starving to death. That the average American took Sunday afternoon drives was not within his realm of belief.

What did the Vietnamese do for pastime? Mostly nothing. They "fiddled around" a lot. A few could play, and many would try to play, a bamboo flute or a guitar or mandolin. Regardless of their talent, most of the sounds they produced were, to me, noise. But then nearly all Vietnamese music was a strain on my nerves. The first time I heard it I was reminded of a basement full of grade school horn-blowers trying to imitate the cry of a panther. And then the wailing would stop, but the respite was not long enough to relieve my headache. Surely, I thought, no composer would dare write this down!

He dared. I heard the same sounds over and over, originating from sheet music that showed the same key signatures and music symbols we have in America. How a single sheet of paper could be the source of so much caterwaul I still don't know.

The "music," whether instrumental or vocal, was uniformly political in nature. There were many military marches played to celebrate the latest victories. Slower tunes reflected sympathy for the "downtrodden underdogs persecuted by obdurate aggressors." I sympathized, too, for the downtrodden underdogs persecuted by obdurate "music."

Vietnamese paintings also portrayed political themes. The displays were mostly in watercolor, charcoal, or red brick, and they were a far cry from the artistic achievements in China or Japan. They resembled exhibits of grade school children.

The people, youngsters and adults alike, played games. A favorite was "cockfight," in which each of the participants held one ankle and hopping on one foot, tried to knock the other person over. Another was "bean bag," in which the players threw their little projectiles at caricatures of President Johnson and later Nixon hung from a tree branch. Volleyball was popular. They also wrote letters and played checkers or chess. Most of all they seemed to enjoy just "lazying."

Once, after our treatment had improved prior to our release, an unusual incident occurred. A new guard—we called him "Babyface"—unlocked our door and entered, leaving the door open behind him. He stood over us and watched us play bridge, seeming to know about trump, the order of face cards, etc. (Incidentally, the Vietnamese were not superstitious about the ace of spades as far as I could tell.) After a hand or two, we POWs decided that we would ask him to join us in a game. He seemed extraordinarily friendly and, with the door open, very vulnerable to severe chastisement if an officer would walk by. Besides, we thought, we might be able to use him sometime.

We gestured to the guard to sit down. To our amazement, he did. We dealt a few hands to play the easiest game we could think of—"Oh hell." This game, while involving luck, requires some skill because the player had to predetermine the number of tricks he would be able to take in each hand.

Thinking that we might be able to win something, we pointed to his pencil, indicating that as a wager.

"No." He didn't want to bet.

Well, how about his broken wristwatch, which dangled from around his neck by a piece of homemade string? (He'd probably taken it from some captured American pilot.)

"No."

Finally we pointed to his boots, still shiny from basic training.

"Oh, no!"

So there were no bets. We passed him the deck. Deftly, he picked it up with his right hand and smoothly dealt the cards counterclockwise and off the bottom of the deck! We were taken aback, but thinking that he was dealing the Vietnamese way we let him continue. After two rounds, he looked up at us and grinned slyly. Then he started passing the rest of the cards in the customary manner.

So "Babyface" was putting us on! We glanced around in wonderment. This guy might be a card shark.

After seven hands, he lagged behind in the score. Only three more hands to go, and the game would be over. The eighth hand, he won. The ninth, he won. The tenth, he won again and ended with the highest score.

With that, he stood up and, poker-faced, picked up our four pairs of rubber-tire sandals, walked out, and locked the door.

We looked at each other unable to speak. A moment later we could no longer contain ourselves, and rollicked on our racks, howling with laughter. Here we were, outhustled by this "naïve" guard who still wore black shiny boots. And there he was, hands full of grubby sandals. We were "tired out"!

Thirty minutes later we were still bursting with uncontrollable guffaws when the guard opened the door, threw back the "tires," locked the door, and left.

For days we revived the card game in our minds and laughed. We also studied the possibility of using "Babyface" for our purposes. It was not to be. Within a week, and apparently after indoctrination, "Babyface" turned 180 degrees and refused to have a thing to do with us. We asked him to join us in cards, but he would not even respond.

Nevertheless, this brief episode was by far the friendliest, and about the only, regard from any V that I experienced in my six years of captivity.

The Vietnamese told jokes and riddles, but they never laughed at themselves or at our jokes. Everything we said was interpreted literally; they simply could not comprehend our use of humorous sarcasm or irony. Belittling oneself for a laugh was unknown to them.

They loved to playact. They pictured themselves as revolutionary leaders, as future Ho Chi Minhs, pompously strutting around carrying political banners or directing others to shoot down American aircraft.

They wanted attention and vainly boasted about their possessions, how far they could throw a rock, or how high they could jump. To me this meant they were insecure and were trying to break away from their own nonentity. Even when they coughed they were as loud and dramatic as they could be. They never tried to hold back. Sneezes could be heard a block away, but the bid for attention fell on indifferent ears.

The Vietnamese rarely exerted themselves. Why should they? If they were going to get a meal at all, they'd eat regardless of whether they "worked" for it. They didn't worry. They didn't have to. The state was responsible for their welfare as well as their guidance. Even the upkeep of state property was not their problem.

To me this was a nation of people with misdirected energies. They teased animals, they threw rocks. They beat birds' nests with sticks. They chatted, they smoked, they dozed.

As is the case with any ethnic group, the Vietnamese make an interesting but complex study. Interpretations and generalizations are admittedly mine, based on thousands of hours of observation. Initially, I often misunderstood Vietnamese behavior or intent. As the years dragged by, however, I became more adept both in my observation and in my understanding, because I was compelled to discover some subtle clue to help me escape or endure my fate. My task was similar to putting together a difficult picture puzzle. Some of the "pieces" of behavior were easy to connect. Some were very deceptive. And some appeared not to fit at all. Standing away for perspective, I can appreciate how specific impressional pieces form a general—although sometimes vague—whole.

The Vietnamese seemed more content than Americans, often smiling and laughing at work and play. Frequently they were childishly giddy and irresponsible. They also carried strains of an unpredictable sadism. They were excitable. They were stoic about pain. Although generally not sentimental, they mourned the death of Ho Chi Minh. They lied and stole from each other but rarely came to fisticuffs. They were vain and ostentatious, but they were afraid.

Once I was asked to carry rice into a storeroom. I entered the room and discovered a Vietnamese girl, the first I'd seen in two years, cornered by a "criminal." She went into hysterics, sobbing and screaming with fright. I don't know what the guards had told her about POWs, but she was certain that I was going to assault her. Guards, following me into the storeroom, laughed and ordered me out. I felt only compassion for the little girl.

A Vietnamese nod of the head means "no." A gesture of open hands sweeping out and reaching forward means "come here." "Me" in Vietnamese means "you." I was in a new ball park, with a new set of signals. It took much time and effort, but I learned to cope with my opposition.

vietnamese construction

In February of 1968 I stepped up on my bunk boards and balanced myself on the windowsill of Pigsty 1—our cell. Curious, I wanted to peek out a four-inch by four-foot ventilation hole on top of a bricked-in "window." To do this was, of course, against the rules; and if I were caught, I would be beaten severely.

I was vulnerable, but I had help. My two roommates were accomplished eavesdroppers themselves and, with a clearing of the throat, could warn me against lurking guards. The three of us had developed a keen sense of smell and could detect odors of cigarettes or "toilet-water" perfume. We were not the least bit enchanted, regardless of the fragrance they selected. This aroma was evidence of their vanity . . . and of their presence.

Pigsty's peephole was an especially good one: I could look out to see Vietnamese civilians pruning their gardens or carrying their chogey poles on the way to market. I would watch for hours—until I could no longer endure the cramped back muscles from prolonged stooping. From the outside I was safe from view. The ventilation hole was about eight feet from the floor, a level too high for the average V to walk by and see in. And it was so close to the perimeter wall of the camp that guards could not back away far enough to attain the necessary angle of vision.

Years earlier, Pigsty provided living quarters for actors and actresses in a complex (which we dubbed the "Zoo") that had been a French film studio. Now we American POWs acted out our own perpetual games of "cat and mouse" or "three little pigs and the big, bad wolf."

I glanced down from the sill as usual and acknowledged my buddies' standard signal—"thumbs up." I peered out.

The Pigsty, resting on higher ground than the perimeter wall, enabled me to see outside the prison camp and into a little valley. In this valley was a pond of water about twenty yards in diameter. I recognized that some of the weeds growing around the pond were the same flora that I had seen floating in our soups.

Behind the pond was a garden patch containing bona fide vegetables—corn, beans, and peas—which I hadn't seen in my soup. Opposite the garden was a main road, lined with buildings. I could see only the backs of these buildings except for one vacant lot. Occasionally peasants would leave the road and run behind the buildings to relieve themselves. Enclosed restrooms were obviously not available; rather, backyards served as undesignated public latrines.

But on this day an unusual event occurred—unusual because up to this time I had seen nothing more therapeutic than a broken bicycle or a chogey pole. A man strolled to the near side of the lot, lugging a tripod under his arm, and I took especial note. He set it up, and squinting through his transit scope started yelling and pointing out increments to his "pole" assistant on the other end of the lot. Red markers were then staked to form a line. What project are they up to now, I wondered. Probably an auxiliary road to divert the already too heavy military traffic.

Peasants, belatedly learning about the construction, trailed the surveyor and hopped spaniel-like into the pond to rescue soup-weeds. Others rushed to pick vegetables, still green, from the patch.

Several days later, water buffalo, probably a hundred of them, lumbered into the barren garden, drawing carts. These carts often were supported by axles of broken jeeps or trucks, and the frames and beds were pieced together with scraps of wood. In the carts were stacked red bricks, similar to those I'd seen in the States, except not so regular or smooth.

I decided to challenge myself by taking an accurate count of the bricks as they were hauled off the carts. It was hopeless: like hurried ants after monsoon rains, peasants from all directions heaped brick upon brick until the pile was eight or nine feet high and about twenty-five yards long. There were hundreds of thousands of them. At the end of the day, the carts were empty, and the buffalo plodded back to unseen stalls. After the dust cleared, I scanned this colossal expanse of red brick and wondered what it would become.

The next day was moving day. Fifty or so Vietnamese climbed the brick mountain and, one by one, carried each brick twelve or fifteen feet, razing one heap to erect another. This surprised me, and I wondered why they spent a full day of time and expense to make this big red "elephant" roll over.

Workmen came the next morning with picks and shovels and started digging a three-foot foundation trench . . . precisely where the original stack of bricks had been. This was the first chapter in my manual on Vietnamese organization.

I was also surprised that the foundation diggers didn't go any deeper than three feet, because the soil they were working with, characteristic of the delta, was sandy and soft. Such a footing seemed insubstantial for a structure utilizing so many bricks.

The Vietnamese manner of digging a foundation was apparently pioneered to reduce unemployment. While one man dug the foundation, twenty men and women on ground level faced each other shoulder to shoulder, forming two lines. The digger took one shovelful of dirt and filled a saucer-shaped wicker basket. The closest member in one of the lines reached down and picked up the basket and handed it not to the person nearest him but across to a fellow in the other line. Then the basket was passed back to the worker standing next to the one who started it all. The little container zigzagged down the lines like a tab to a zipper and the dirt was dumped into a pile only fifteen feet from its origin. The dirt could have been thrown this far from the digger's shovel!

Another team of diggers concentrated on a circular hole which I thought was going to be a well. When it was about ten feet deep, the diggers crawled out and carts were pulled to the opening. In the carts was a loose, white, powdery substance—lye—and the diggers started using it to fill the hole. Acrid dust permeated the air, and fifty yards away I could hardly breathe. How much longer could these people shovel before they got sick? That lye must have seared their eyes.

Finally the "hole" was full, and next to it cartloads of sand were unloaded. It was time to make mortar, and mixers hauled water from the pond, threw it on the ground, added sand and straw and lye, stirred it with a hoe, and scooped it into a bucket. Now construction could begin.

The bricklayers were older men who wore a kind of tam-o-shanter hat, long-sleeved shirts, ragged trousers, and no footwear. They seemed to command much respect from the other workers.

As the bricks rose to shoulder height, it was necessary to build scaffolds. These were constructed entirely from bamboo, tied together with homemade ropes. Even if steel had been available, the peasants would not have used it to build scaffolds because they did not trust steel. (I would not have trusted their bamboo!) Pole was braced to pole, and then the bracings were rebraced until the scaffolding resembled a labyrinthine bamboo jungle.

Rough boards were placed on the bracing as platforms for the bricklayers. The higher the walls, the higher the subsequent platforms, until the mortar mixers could no longer reach up to put a bucket on the boards. Consequently, the bricklayers dropped fibrous ropes, and the mixers fastened them to handles of their refilled buckets.

The sole tool of the bricklayer looked like a kitchen cleaver. With its dull edge the mason broke the bricks, nudged them into place, picked up a glob of mortar, slapped it on the top line of bricks, and scraped off the excess.

Being the son of a carpenter and having laid a few bricks and blocks myself, I was appalled at the primitive construction techniques still employed in North Viet Nam. These people had so little to work with, but they seemed to utilize effectively everything they had.

When the wall reached an elevation of about eight feet the bricklayer patterned a four- or five-foot opening with the jagged bricks jutting out into the space. Clearly this was going to be a window. Carpenters climbed the scaffolding and, with chisels and saws, smoothed the bricks and assembled a wooden frame. Four days later, the carpenters completed three windows (on the side that I could observe) and painted the frames a deep shade of green. This was the most professional work that I had seen so far.

But the boss came. He puttered around, gazed toward the windows, and initiated a ruckus. Disconsolate carpenters lagged behind, humbled and hurt. The boss stomped away.

That afternoon, the carpenters returned, not with their customary chisels and saws, but with a bricklayer's cleaver and a piece of metal—their hammer—which had been pilfered from a downed American aircraft. Eventually three new holes were knocked out of the solid brick wall. Picking up the fallen pieces the carpenters started to mortar in the original holes. They recklessly splintered the carefully fitted wooden frames. Not until nightfall was the last brick chipped to size and cemented in.

The next morning the carpenters—again with their own tools—began the process of reframing the new windows. As was the case when the bricks were first stacked, this was another example of grand organization in construction. The carpenters had not read their instructions, nor had the bricklayers. I doubt that they could have: there weren't any instructions to read.

The building grew and grew, and I began to question whether it would ever have a covering. I also wondered how a roof was to be added because up to this point I had not seen one hint of construction machinery. When the walls were twenty feet high the bricklayers carved notches into the crest. Then the peasants hauled beams—the support for the roof's frame—up the scaffolding and slipped them into the gaps.

Oxen approached, straining under the weight of timbers

six inches square and thirty feet long. With hand tools, the workers drilled and cut the lumber to structure four triangular frames. Men then dragged them into the building. Through the windows I could still see what was happening.

Some of the workers left to muster all of the peasants they could find, and soon a couple hundred were charging around the base, crawling up and down the scaffolding, yelling and screaming and trying to out-supervise one another. With bamboo poles and homemade ropes they twisted and turned until the frames were hoisted to the top. After much grunting and grimacing they turned the frames upright. Finally, a long timber was placed across the four A-frames.

At this point—for the first and only time—I saw a construction tool: a wrench to tighten a fourteen-inch stove bolt driven through holes in the beams.

Carpenters gingerly snaked up the bolted beams and nailed vertical strips of bamboo to the slanted roof. Several days later they secured horizontal strips and set tile on top of them.

The building was, after three months, "complete."

Up to this time none of us knew the purpose of this new structure. One obvious clue, however, came when eight smokestacks arose above the far wall. By means of our underground network system, we tapped out this new information and established a contest to determine who could guess the building's function. Speculation ran the gamut—from "crematorium" to "whorehouse."

About a week later the long-awaited answer came. An oxcart rambled up with a load of coal dust. With one big black cloud, the dust was dumped onto the ground. Vietnamese peasants gathered around the pile, squatted on their haunches, and, adding water and mud to the dust, packed the coal into balls. These black "snowballs" were then set in the sun to dry.

I had seen this process before. In fact, I had made thousands of these coal balls myself. This was the only fuel the prison's cooks used to sterilize our water and to heat our food. Loose coal dust would not ignite and all of the hard coal was going to the war effort, especially to freight trains carrying supplies to the front.

We knew these balls weren't for heating the building, because it was April. The V were going to bake something. The next morning's gong awakened us to a smoke-filled valley. The eight smokestacks were huffing and puffing pungent carbon particles. Even in this contaminated air, however, isolated molecules of a discreet and delicate scent reached our nostrils. Fresh-baked bread—so close that we could almost grab a loaf!

But it was no use. Not once did the Vietnamese come to Pigsty 1 to deliver any orders. With straw and sticks and stones, the "big, bad wolf" had built a place of his own.

11

vietnamese propaganda

Ho Chi Minh understood well the two elements necessary to maintain totalitarian control, and he stressed them time and again: agitation and propaganda. His constituency, no longer able to bear its sordid living conditions, was already agitated. It was the business of the Minister of Propaganda to channel that anger and frustration to an external scapegoat. He did this by manipulating the minds of the people.

From the powerful Ministry came encompassing "truths"—policies, news, general information. These controlled "truths" were the lifeblood of communism. One of the government publications quoted a man saying, "I'm so happy that I'm free to condemn the past and to glorify the revolution." To me, that statement typified the Vietnamese concept of freedom. These people were free to condemn the American system, but not to examine it objectively. They were free to glorify the revolution, but never free to curse it.

Radio broadcasts were the primary sources of propaganda—for peasants and POWs alike. Hamlets, no matter how remote, could not escape the rebounding echoes of a Ho Chi Minh speech or a military march. When I was moved from camp to camp, I saw villages which were absolutely destitute—no water or sewage system, no secure shelter, no electricity. No electricity, that is, except for a single strand of wire strung around bushes and branches and bamboo poles leading to a shining multi-kilowatt speaker often as large as eight feet in diameter.

During the U.S. strikes on Hanoi in 1972 we were moved out of the city to a distant jungle camp. I'll never forget our return to Hoa Lo (Hanoi Hilton), crossing the Red River for the last time, and knowing that the end of the war was near.

The bridges over the river had been bombed, and we had to cross the mile-wide waters on rickety pontoons. Leaving the river, we saw monstrous loudspeakers, the source of blaring music which shattered the humid silence for miles. It was eerie. Three huge speakers, looming omnipotent, broadcast the same harangue that I had endured for six years. Even the forbidding jungles granted no deliverance from the propaganda.

Sign-on time for V radio programs was usually 5:00 a.m., depending on whether the radio "technician" awakened on schedule. Broadcasting stopped for about three hours at 11:00 a.m. for siesta time and blared again until late at night. Saturdays' bombasts lasted until one or two the following morning, with stirring marches and speeches and what sounded like melodramas.

The broadcast amplification was so ear-splitting that even though I was fifty yards away I suffered frequent headaches. Hapless peasants were also victims, their shacks often the support for the booming iron throats.

The Ministry of Propaganda designed a program

especially for American soldiers in South Viet Nam and for POWs. This very poor imitation of Voice of America was extremely loud, and "as cannons overcharged with double cracks," the two battling broadcasts, in English and in Vietnamese, racked our auditory systems. Often the fidelity was so poor that we couldn't understand their stuttered "pidgin" English. With speakers outside every POW cell, however, we had no way to control the volume or the program selection. Even when the camp had no power, auxiliary generators were quickly tied in so that we would not be without "listening entertainment."

The POW programs started at 6:00 a.m. and lasted for thirty minutes, and the same charade was rerun from 9:00 to 9:30 p.m. Three V girls (with names that sounded like Tuzoom, KeyMy, and Von Soon) mimicked the style of Tokyo Rose in World War II. Appropriately, we named them "Hanoi Hannah." (At first, these girls really "turned us off," but the longer we listened, the better they sounded—not because of *what* they said, but because they were *female voices.*)

Obviously, the daily broadcasts included countless variations, but a rendering of the programming went like this:

This is the voice of Viet Nam. This is the voice of Viet Nam, broadcasting from Hanoi, capital of the Democratic Republic of Viet Nam. Our program in English is broadcast daily at 600, 1200, 1500, and 2100 hours. [The programs were sent to GIs in South Viet Nam, and we were usually spared the noon and afternoon broadcasts.]
Here are the headlines:
... Twenty thousand American troops wiped out by one guerrilla company.
... One hundred fifty thousand demonstrators show increasing anti-war attitude of American people.
... Ninety-fifth session of Paris Conference held today proved the bankrupt policy of the American capitalist warmongers.

And now for the program in detail. . . .

On the battlefield, in an extraordinary display of courage, sure and certain victories were won by guerrilla fighters. [The North Vietnamese never admitted having Viet Cong or Regulars in the South. Rather, their soldiers were referred to as one of three kinds of "liberation fighters": guerrillas, hamlet fighters, or regional fighters.]

Three hundred kilometers north-northeast of Saigon, near the small village De Dak Bot, three enemy camps were overrun and completely decimated by the brave and brilliant action of Regional Fighter Troupe 409. By very accurate planning and skillful employment of rudimentary weapons, they were able to overcome with little more than spears and hoes the far higher number of American soldiers supported by artillery, armor, and fighter planes.

On the early morning of 14 August, before the Yankees awakened, Troupe 409 encircled the camps and with great accuracy caught by complete surprise the entire enemy encampment.

The commander of one camp is reported to have shouted out to his men: "Save himself who can!" but the soldiers had nowhere to hide. One captured American soldier was found underneath his bed, crying uncontrollably.

The number of enemy soldiers killed so far this month, according to incomplete figures, is 314,226. The sovereign nation of Viet Nam will acquire the ultimate victory over perfidious aggressors and obdurate fascist-capitalists.

Special praise must go to eighty-two-year-old Mok Chi Bin who, with one shell from her muzzle-loaded musket, shot ablaze an F105 Thunderchief. On Wednesday, this valiant fighter and defender of the fatherland will receive the Second Class Hero Award and the Valiant Destroyer of Yanks Award.

And now, news from home. . . .

Over 150,000 demonstrators marched up and down Market Street in San Francisco Sunday, protesting the filthy war in Viet Nam. They carried placards and banners which read "Johnson—withdraw!" and "Stop the needless bloodshed!" Thousands of people lined the streets and demanded that the genocide cease.

A brave and valiant American student, doused with gasoline, set himself ablaze to dramatize the unfeeling cruelty of perfidious capitalist warmongers. Next Saturday, we will dedicate our new Thai Nguyen brass ball-bearing factory in his honor.

[Tragedies in America warranted frequent coverage in V broadcasts. News concentrated on plane crashes, riots, and killings. The assassinations of Bobby Kennedy and Martin Luther King, Jr., were reported for months as "typical debacles, an example of American respect for leadership."]

And now, to the valiant fighters of Army 603, we dedicate this song entitled "Pull Out His Liver." [Believe it or not, that was a popular tune. To the Oriental jungle fighter it was a practice (although not openly condoned) to extract the liver of an enemy soldier and eat it. This cannibalistic ritual provided nourishment to starving guerrillas.]

And now, world news. . . .

Mr. Le Duc Tho spoke at the ninety-seventh session in Paris today and renounced the United States for its perfidious schemes in trying to make black, white. He proved once and for all that the American negotiators have been trying to confuse in the minds of the world's people the real identity of the aggressor and the victims of aggression. Mr. Duc Tho convincingly established the fact that the American imperialists will never win in Viet Nam because the powers of the world support the Vietnamese cause. Useless efforts to deny this fact by American spokesmen were scorned by all who were present.

And now, to the workers of the Xom Trong bicycle factory who increased their production over 200 percent in two months, we dedicate this song: "Shoot Straight at the Aggressors."

[North Vietnamese workers were frequently referred to as "The Great Rear," corresponding to V.C. soldiers who were "The Great Front." Needless to say, we made more than a few jokes about this. One of the V negotiators, M. Nguyen T. Binh (we called her "Win D Bag"), was once reported to have "Laid it bare on the table, glorifying her Great Rear."]

[Hannah, using a tone of voice she thought was sexy, continued with melancholy violin music in the background.]

GIs, why fight this illegal, immoral, unjust war in South Viet Nam? You know that huge corporations in your country are making napalm and that their profits are getting higher and higher while our babies burn to death. Don't you see the truth? Don't you know that you are participants in an unjust, immoral war? Give up before you, too, have to die a useless death.

And now, for those who died—but not for their fatherland. [She followed the statement with fifteen or twenty names of infantrymen and a pilot or two—American GIs who had been killed in action. POWs listened in dreadful fear of hearing the name of a brother or buddy fighting in the South.]

[The V never admitted their own military casualties, mentioning only that Hanoi had been hit and that many civilian women and children had been killed. During an interrogation I once asked the officer why their casualties were never reported. With surprising candor he answered: "We could not otherwise keep the people enthusiastic about the war."]

* * *

Once a week two anti-war Americans sent a tape of a show, of poor quality by American standards but done well in the eyes of the Vietnamese. Generally the tape included American music and gave a review of sports events. The program, called "Special Broadcast from Home," was not designed for prisoners but rather for our guys in South Viet Nam. We frequently were not allowed to hear these broadcasts.

Immediately after the Son Tay attempt to free the prisoners in the the winter of 1970, all POWs were moved into Hanoi for security reasons. The V squeezed fifty-seven prisoners into a 25- by 35-foot cell. Although we had no more than fourteen inches of bed space apiece, we were overjoyed to be among comrades.

The first day we were given no water or food. The second and third days our meals were dried fish, stale bread, and water. Hunger stuck in our throats, but the same hour we arrived, officers provided the basic communist necessity— propaganda. A guard crawled up to the roof with wires for a radio speaker. This was a typical example of the V enthusiasm to feed our minds.

Some of our guys became very upset about the speakers. They didn't listen, and they didn't want any other POW to listen. They thought it would poison our minds. A few POWs believed they could learn something from the broadcasts by listening between the lines. Occasionally, brief verbal flare-ups arose.

Initially I too was deeply concerned about the V's attempt to brainwash me, but those concerns were soon dispelled. The radio broadcasts, like propaganda, were so ludicrous that they provided many laughs. However, included in their absurdities were subtle indicators, enabling us to detect the turn of Vietnamese war morale.

The radio broadcasts orignated from a main office somewhere. Not infrequently, the jughead technician would turn on the amplifier before he had made his program selection.

One of the biggest thrills of my long captivity occurred just before Christmas in 1967. The V technician had turned on the amplifiers and heard music. He was too naïve to recognize that it was a beautiful American carol—"The Little Drummer Boy"—and allowed it to continue to completion. After the song, he heard an announcement in English—it was the Voice of America! I cried.

A similar incident happened several years later. It was a cold, dreary day; my cellmate and I, our teeth chattering, were bundled up in rags and thin blankets. All of a sudden we heard Ray Charles singing "What'd I Say?" Both of us jumped up as though we had been resurrected from the dead, shed our blankets, and started twisting.

Insecure, the Vietnamese felt compelled to censure their own broadcasts. On several occasions they forgot about the headline announcement at the beginning of the program. For example, one headline stated: "American pilot speaks out against the war." We listened carefully.

It was no use. Instead of the news story, we had two minutes of dead air. We later told some of the more intelligent V senior officers, "We know you're playing admissions of tortured American pilots. Why don't you just let us hear what they have to say?"

The V lost face, and the broadcasts were stopped for several days.

Every few weeks we received a newspaper written in English called the *Viet Nam Courier*. It was ten or twelve pages in length, and filled with propaganda. Articles that failed to pass censorship were occasionally inked out; sometimes entire pages were omitted. Two weeks after I was shot down I saw a picture of my RIO Gary Anderson and one of me taken as we had "let people see face."

The newspaper contained fantastic stories. One heralded a great husband-wife team of freedom fighters. This valiant couple, destined to save their fatherland, overcame extreme hardships. The only weapons in their armory were two bows and one arrow, and with these the pair developed a rapid-fire technique. To do this, the wife awakened each morning and wrapped her long hair into a bun atop her head. She climbed a tree along a path and waited for unsuspecting GIs. When one came along, she released her only arrow and struck the soldier. Her husband came out of hiding, retrieved the arrow, and shot it back to his wife—right into her bun! That technique required extreme accuracy on the part of the husband . . . and much faith on the part of the wife! But it was a story no American could believe.

Another article described the "apple-core" shot. Because he was always without adequate ammunition, one freedom fighter developed a method to kill four or five Americans with one bullet. When Americans ran helter-skelter for their lives, he stood poised until several of them were lined up down his gunsight. Then he shot his rifle so that the bullet passed through all of them. The newspaper described this as a widespread technique and announced that its developer achieved the "Second Class Hero" award.

An article which received front-page headlines showed pictures of how a man had trained hornets to attack GIs. The photographs depicted the V soldier in a field with scarecrows dressed in GI uniforms. The trainer pointed with a flag the direction he wanted the hornets to fly. Accounts reported that in actual battle the hornets had stunned and even killed American soldiers.

One special news release that ran for a week with extraordinary ballyhoo backfired. In early spring of 1970, the Mekong River Delta area near Cambodia was in turmoil. Communist newspapers and radio broadcasts reported:

> The U.S.S. *Columbia Eagle* has mutinied. Anti-war sailors have taken control of the freighter and have brought their shipload of arms and munitions into Sihanoukville, port city of Cambodia. These American sailors have handed over large quantities of war supplies to Vietnamese freedom fighters. Sure and certain victory for the oppressed peoples in Indochina is near.

We were appalled that the North Vietnamese could even think of mutiny on an American ship. But the headlines continued throughout the week: "American Sailors Support National Liberation Front."

At the end of the week, however, another account of the incident appeared:

> A clique of traitors, henchmen of U.S. imperialist aggressors and puppets of the Nixon regime, have sneaked into Cambodia's capital city, Phnom Penh, and in a coup d'etat have illegally taken control of the government. F.U.N.K. fighters [Fighters of the United National Kingdom] tried desperately to retake the capital city and to reestablish the proper authority of Prince Norodom Sihanouk. They were unable to defend the city because imperialist aggressors had utilized a huge cache of weapons secretly smuggled in from a freighter called the U.S.S. *Columbia Eagle*.

One of the most tragic stories from the *Courier* was an account of a five-year-old boy who was posthumously given the "Valiant Destroyer of Yanks" award. A platoon of GIs were milling around their camp, smoking cigarettes and telling stories when a little boy, wearing ragged shirt and pants, scampered from his village, approached the GIs, and yelled the only English he knew: "Hey, GI, you got gum?" Ten or twelve GIs reached into their pockets for gum and candy and squatted around the youngster to watch him enjoy it. At that moment, a plastic mine, strapped to the chest of the child, exploded, splattering him and the GIs over the countryside.

This child was depicted by the *Courier* as having made the ultimate sacrifice for the Vietnamese cause—as if he could understand that cause. Compassionate American soldiers were killed. Those soldiers who watched their buddies get blown up must have felt a very different emotion the next time they heard, "Hey, GI, you got gum?"

A twenty-page Vietnamese magazine entitled *Viet Nam* was distributed to POWs three or four times a year. It had no date or volume number, but it did contain pictures, many of which were so black that we could not discern any features. Stories, with numerous printing errors, were always revolutionary. The magazine did occasionally show the latest commemorative stamp or include a book review. Unusually honest, the editors appealed: "Dear Reader, we know that this magazine has many errors and is of low quality. We request your help. If you find errors, please tell us so that we can improve."

Near the end of the war, the Vietnamese made a concerted effort to upgrade our treatment. Officials wanted wide coverage of POWs playing volleyball, chess, or eating "good" food. The Vietnamese government also wanted to make us feel that this improved treatment was representative. They felt they could make us forget all our suffering, but we had better memories than their peasants.

For the first time in six years I was allowed to gather with all the other prisoners in the camp courtyard, for exercise or volleyball. We soon discovered, however, that photographers were hiding behind "duck blinds" made from trees or bamboo screens. We predetermined that, as soon as any one of us saw suspicious feet or heard the whirring of cameras, he would shout out the code word "Kodak." Then all POWs would stop whatever they were doing and return to their cells.

A few days before our release, the senior officers were called into a V office and told: "We want to send you off with good tidings. To show our goodwill, we have arranged to present to you a show performed by our country's foremost entertainers. We will bring to you Trung Vy, who is known throughout the world for her beautiful voice." (The idea probably originated from their knowing how popular the Bob Hope shows were in the South.)

Our officers, realizing the dangerous propaganda potential, answered: "We are not interested in seeing your show, but thank you anyway. We'd rather just wait in our rooms until we are released." For several days, the negotiations continued. On 9 February oxcarts loaded with backdrops, lighting, costumes, etc., entered the prison and stopped near the bath area. It took the V a full day to chip out large holes in the concrete paving for stage supports.

Tension increased as it became more and more apparent that the V camp commander had assured his high officials that this show would be successful and that pictures would be taken of laughing and applauding prisoners. Still, our answer was *no*.

V officials visited cells individually and personally invited each POW to attend. We were fully aware that this supreme effort was engineered by a war-torn, unsophisticated nation which needed to brighten a tarnished image of POW treatment. We remained unified. We were not going to leave our rooms.

The performers arrived, including attractive girls. They dressed in their costumes and rehearsed. That evening the show began. I could hear Trung Vy's lovely voice and, curious, I wanted to watch the performance. But the price of admission was too great.

Three hours later, the dancing stopped and the last verse was sung. The gala event was complete. But there was no curtain call. The "audience" had already gone to bed.

The next morning the guards let us go into the courtyard. It was a cold, gray, misty morning, and Ed Davis and I watched the troupe tear down the stage. The young girls hustled to the carts with their costumes. A more pensive lady, followed by an interpreter, paused to talk with Ed and me. It was Trung Vy.

With sad face, she asked through her interpreter, "Why you not listen me sing?" Ed responded, "You'll have to ask your leaders." The V leaders always told the people that we had admitted our sins and had accepted and loved them as our friends. They were wrong. I imagine that singing to hanging laundry was the greatest humiliation Trung Vy had ever experienced. I felt pity for her as she left with tears in her eyes.

As early as 1970 the V had started construction of a 150-foot-high communications tower. They told us that when they had driven the last aggressor from their soil, they would triumphantly hoist their national banner to this majestic point.

On 27 January 1973 a huge North Vietnamese flag (a five-pointed gold star centered on red background) was carried up the tower by a V soldier. An astute—and cocky—American POW approached V officials and asked, "What's the story on the flag?"

"Oh, you not know? We wait many year put up flag celebrate our victory over most powerful member aggressive Western imperialist camp. Beautiful symbol, no?"

The POW muttered something under his breath and walked off. Thirty minutes later, the same weary soldier reclimbed the tower to undo his mistake. The "beautiful symbol" was upside down!

comm net

For two weeks after my capture I waited alone in my cell, reconstructing the events which were to have such a tremendous impact on my life and Anne's. I relived the thump of the missile, the ejection, the encounter with angry peasants, the jarring ride to town, the interrogations, the torture. I remembered the photographers who wanted to tell me something but didn't dare. I saw purple on skin which was white the day before. I replayed the broken English of the V officer telling me how I would "leeve in peace" merely by observing camp regulations.

The harsh reality made any optimism seem contrived. Camp rules threatened my hope. The hours seemed interminable, yet there was not enough time for me to comprehend the situation well enough to prepare for the future. Open prison compounds were nowhere in sight. Nothing matched the "expert's" classroom description of what to expect if I were shot down.

How long will this last? Do any of the other prisoners have cellmates? What about Regulation Number Ten: "Criminals must not communicate with or look at other criminals in other rooms or outside"? Did prisoners have an underground communication system? If so, how could I hook in to it?

After about a week, the guard gave me two cigarettes with my meal. I didn't smoke, and I decided to leave them at the sewage hole where POWs emptied their *bo*'s (sewage buckets) each morning. When it was my turn to dump my *bo*, I walked to the open cistern with the cigarettes hidden under my waistband. The guard did not follow me into the area, probably because it reeked of feces and ammonia, and the air was blackened by flies. I slipped the cigarettes out and concealed them near a rock, dumped the bucket, and left.

The next day the cigarettes were gone. I replaced them. Each day thereafter they disappeared. I knew that the other POWs had found my "drop" and that rudimentary communication had been established. This simple act was extremely important to me; once again I could join in fellowship with other Americans, no matter how remote. Even the heavier footsteps of unseen comrades brought great comfort as do innocent snores of a dad to an anxious child.

One night as I was sitting on my bunk the silence was interrupted by the chirping of a cricket. I paid little attention because my cell was often occupied by rats, lizards, and insects. A half minute later I recognized that this cricket had a particular rhythm to its chirp. The little bug was obviously educated, so I went to the corner to investigate. I looked down, and what I saw was not a cricket at all but a wire protruding from a little hole close to the dirty floor.

Again the wire scratched on the floor and made more chirping sounds. I watched it intently for two or three minutes and wondered what it could mean. Was it a guard or an American? I decided to peek under the door to see if soldiers were in the area. No one was outside.

Gritting my teeth and trying to bolster all the self-confidence I could, I went back to the wire. It moved again. The room next to mine was vacant, a storeroom for tools, boxes, and ropes. Whatever was moving that wire must be in that room. I had to find out.

With my back to the wall, I dropped my skivvies and pretended to use the *bo,* reached behind me, and tugged three times on the wire. The wire tugged back three times. I tugged four times. It tugged back four times. I tugged five times. It disappeared.

Nothing happened. With sweat dripping off my face, I returned to my bunk and waited for the onslaught of V soldiers. It was very quiet. Fifteen minutes later, back came the wire. This time it had a piece of toilet paper tied to it. I unfolded it and found these words:

"Memorize code.
Eat note."

The code was easier to memorize than the note was to eat, but I did both. I rechecked the door, sat back down on the honey bucket, and tugged on the wire.

The code was a series of tugs which represented letters of the alphabet. The first series indicated the row; the second, the column. The letter "C" was also "K." "M" was therefore transformed to tug, tug, tug . . . tug, tug.

A B C D E
F G H I J
L M N O P
Q R S T U
V W X Y Z

Applying this code, I soon learned that on the other end of the wire was Bob Shumaker who had been shot down two and one half years before I'd checked in. By piecing together bits of wire he had made this communication link, worked it through a crevice in his wall, manipulated it around the boxes and tools and ropes and into the hole in my wall fourteen feet away. This arduous task symbolized his hunger for information. Any tidbits about the States—life-styles, World Series, space program, etc.—became food for his starving mind.

For me, tugging the wire was the second of dozens of techniques I would learn to use in our clandestine communications network. Six years later I would be an expert, capable of giving instruction from firsthand experience.

* * *

In 1968 and in a different camp I heard a cough. I asked my cellmate Robert Wideman to check the door, and I climbed up to the vent. Outside, a POW gestured with his hands, and at first I couldn't understand what he meant. I soon determined that he was forming each letter of the alphabet with his fingers. After he identified the letters a second time, a guard came too close and he had to leave.

The next day, I heard the cough again. By this time I'd memorized the code and could "talk" back. We listed names of the sick and injured POWs, transmitted information about the camp, and finally exchanged the question: "Where U from?"

He spelled out: "K . . . A . . . N . . . S . . . A . . . S."

"What school?"

"S . . . H . . . A . . W . . . N . . . E . . . E . . . M . . . I . . . S . . . S . . . I . . . O . . . N." Ten thousand miles from home, and I couldn't get away from another Kansas Citian!

What a pleasure it was to move in with Captain Ed

Hubbard a year later! We were not only from the same town and high school, but I had graduated with his wife! For weeks we scratched on the floor with bricks every detail we could remember about our city and state. Two years later, we still added details and discovered more mutual acquaintances.

The tap code was easily adapted to other methods besides pulling wire. When we cultivated our weed garden, we struck our hoes to the ground in coded rhythm. We occasionally had to pack dirt and could therefore tamp out messages that traveled a block away. Everyone could hear, but the V never listened. Still, the ramming of that pole to the ground in a neat cadence made us feel as though we were the center of attraction.

The V snapped their wet clothes after the wash, and we did too—in code. We also tied knots in the clothesline. These tactics were obviously slow because we could not be popping our shirts and tying knots all day. The twelve-snap signal it took to spell out my initials was no easy routine. In a span of two months, however, we could relay quite a message with two or three letters a day.

Whenever we were allowed into the courtyard, we knew fifty pairs of American eyes were focused on us. As many as twenty cells faced the sewage hole, and for two hours each day we watched the guards lead the prisoners two by two to dump their *bo*'s. The POWs often "shot the bird" to what were only doors to the naïve guards.

The most common use of the tap code was our pounding of knuckles or a small piece of wood on the mortared walls. The listener on the opposite side pressed his ear flush to the mortar. After years of practice, we communicated messages from one end of the building to the other within a half hour.

Nonetheless, we still could improve. After analyzing the system carefully, I decided the tap code wasted a lot of time.

After all, the frequently used letter "T" required eight taps. I knew it would be difficult to implement a new code, but I considered it a worthwhile effort. We could capitalize on the Morse code by rapping the fingertips to signal a dash and tapping a knuckle for a dot.

Nearly all the POWs had at one time learned the Morse code, so it took little effort to refresh their memories. A ham radio operator in grade school, I knew the advantages it could offer. It didn't take much demonstration to show that this code was faster and clearer (it included punctuation). Some of the POWs who were not as involved with communications continued using the accustomed tap code, but those of us who were most active soon rapped messages from room to room faster than a person could write them down.

However, we continued to use the more widely known tap code to make initial contacts with new POWs. We also used it to signal flashes through one vent hole to another across the courtyard. To do this, we stood on a cellmate's shoulders and waved a light piece of material or a white porcelain cup. The cells were often so dark that receivers could not see, and on several occasions we used the flame of a candle made from rendered pork fat and a rag wick. The fellow on the bottom, called the "horse," really took a beating, especially during the hot summer months. When a guard approached a cell, a POW at the door coughed a danger signal and the "horse" immediately dropped to his knees. The communicator then slid silently down his back and on to the floor before the guard could open the door flap. Because "horses" had to brace themselves by planting their hands on the wall, it wasn't long before the telltale smudges evidenced our activity. To avoid this, horses pressed toilet paper between their hands and the walls.

If the vent was big enough, we used the hand code that

Ed Hubbard had taught me. His two-hand system was cumbersome though, because we often had to use one hand to brace ourselves. As a result, we developed a faster one-hand method and saved the two-hand technique for greater distances. Sometimes our cells were in one long building and we used pieces of mirrors to flash signals down the line.

The V coughed and wheezed and spat all the time, and they didn't seem to care if we did the same thing. We decided if we were going to make noise, it might as well mean something. Thus, a series of coughs, sneezes, spits, and wheezes denoted the alphabet or abbreviated words. Each morning it was humorous to hear sniff, hawk, spit: "Good morning! How are you?"

In 1968, after extensive experimentation, we discovered an easier way to pass information through the walls. The problem was to yell loud enough to be heard and yet not alert the guard. The solution was to place the base of our drinking cups to the wall and to press our cheeks tightly into the mouth of the cup so that its lip aligned just under the nose and around the chin. We placed our hands around our cheeks so that no air escaped and then talked into the cup. For the listener, the result was a tinny, nasal message which required much concentration and some experience to understand. It also necessitated toilet tissue to avoid sweaty ear marks.

Before it could become our post office, the sewage hole needed mail. Since we were given no writing materials, we consequently had to devise our own. Ink, for example, was made from ashes or, in the later years, medicines, especially mercurochrome, tincture of violet, and brown diarrhea pills. We also used berries whenever we had access to them. Paint scraped from door frames and mixed with saliva was another

concoction. We used our own blood if we had nothing else, but generally found it illegible after it dried.

For pens we used feathers—if we could find them. Most often pens were made from pieces of metal sneaked in from the trash-ridden courtyard and filed down with a brick or on the cement floor; this procedure sometimes required several months. For handles, we used pieces of bamboo. It was necessary to mate the pen to the ink, cutting a wider slit through the metal for the thicker ash ink. And then the device had to be mated to the absorbent toilet paper by regulating the viscosity of the ink.

On several occasions I was able to steal a pencil or pen during my interrogation. Once an officer sat opposite me with his elbows resting on the tabletop. He opened a junky drawer to show me a picture of anti-war demonstrators in the States. On my stool I sat very close to the table, squeezed my hand up through the gap at the back of the drawer and probed for a pencil. I found one, slowly removed it from the drawer, and hid it under my waistband. Officers would be astounded that Americans could perform such sleight of hand.

Oddly, the guards never punished me for stealing— probably because theft was a Vietnamese life-style. Moreover, the V would lose face to admit that I could filch from their drawers. Once I stole a pencil and hid it in a hole underneath my bunk. I tied a thread to the pencil, lowered it into the hole and threw dirt over the opening. I planned to fish the thread out with a stick and retrieve the pencil.

Guards entered to inspect the cell. Being very thorough, they discovered the hole and consequently the pencil. I was frightened of possible reprisals, knowing that in my possession was high contraband. But I was really irritated—I had spent so much time winning this little trophy.

Undaunted, I stepped up to the officer and exclaimed: "I want my pencil back!"

Aghast at my audacity, he stood speechless for several seconds. Finally he muttered a weak "Not now" and left.

* * *

Delivery of the notes was sometimes very difficult. If the cell blocks were distant, we tied the note to a rock and heaved it "airmail" to the other courtyard. In one instance, the airmail package dropped short of its target and out of our reach. For several hours we prayed that a guard would not notice. Finally a POW was able to edge beyond the usual limits and kick the rock close enough for us to reach it.

Prisoners often delivered notes inside food. Hollowed bread or potatoes were our carrier pigeons. We also stuck notes to the bottom of soup pots with mud or soap and wrote messages with our aluminum spoons on the bottoms of plates. Prisoners who were escorted to the kitchen to wash the dishes collected and read our copy. Utilizing the dishwashers was beautiful when we needed rapid campwide distribution or wanted to establish communications with another cellblock.

The information we passed varied widely. Of immediate concern were the arrivals and departures of POWs. A prisoner leaving the camp generally meant that other POWs would soon be moved. We needed advance warning to collect our contraband and to hide it on our person in case we too had to leave.

Torture of a POW was also important subject matter, especially when the torture indicated a tightening of camp regulations. Most often, however, our communication was simply a morale builder.

A typical note-passing procedure went like this. Late at night I sneaked out all my writing materials and composed messages on paper the size of a matchbook. I folded them carefully so that the ash ink would not come off. The next morning, before the POWs dumped their *bo*'s, I hid these notes under my waistband and peeked through a crack in the door. (Never once in six years was I unable to find a way to see out. Even with especially tight doors, I found that I could perceive motion on the other side by pouring a little water on the floor and using it as a reflector.)

Out walked Jack Van Loan, carrying the bucket with his *left* hand; this meant he was going to *leave* a note. In about thirty minutes, it would be my turn.

When the guard opened my door, I bowed deeply, picked up the bucket with my left hand and walked to the hole, aware that Van Loan was watching. The inattentive guard kicked rocks and pounded the butt of his rifle while I stepped in to the *bo* dump, gagging from the overpowering stench.

I checked my mailbox—a little hole in the bricks covered with a rock—slipped Van Loan's note into my waistband, and at the same time dropped my note behind a rafter above one of the stanchions. After emptying the *bo* I carried it back to my cell with my *right* hand, acknowledging that I had *received* his note.

The contents of the notes took this appearance: My note:

VLN How mate's pegs?
RSL Q. W. Rat
Rat sa hi ranker
Cum camp soon
Tk. MaB. dele.
No bombs 17 days
Tk Pres stop bomb
this area Wt. u. tk?
       JAZ

Van Loan's cellmate, Read Mecleary, was my Annapolis classmate, and I knew he had bad knees. Kay Russell, my cellmate, had just returned from an interrogation by a V officer we called "Rat." Russell learned that a high officer or perhaps a delegation would come soon to inspect the camp. Tk: think. I used JAZ for my initials because it resembled Chas. but was still unidentifiable by the V.

The next morning Van Loan left this note:

JAZ-Wife hurt but no	Van Loan's cellmate (wife was Annapolis
req. for med. V dig	jargon for roommate) has pain in legs, but
new well our end. Tk.	has not requested medicine.
new bath. Truck camp	A truck entered camp last night, perhaps
l.n. MaB new guys	to put new POWs in Corncrib, another
corncrib Good wx—	building in the prison.
no bombs. V in trubs.	Weather is good, but still no bombs.
Must talk soon.	We'll be home by Christmas.
Get urs under tre.	
VLN	

Sometimes we waited a week or ten days before we picked up or dropped our next notes, depending on how closely the guard watched and if we'd had a chance to write. Occasionally, the note was misplaced.

We had only five or six seconds to place the note through the flies. Once I found a note which had been misplaced a few inches. I took it to my cell and read:

N.G. WH4	New guy—Warehouse 4
Bowling?	Name—Bowling?

The note referred to POW Bailey who had moved into Warehouse 4 six months earlier!

Unlike stealing, communicating with another POW was grounds for severe punishment. We took extreme chances swapping notes. If we were about to be caught we "accidentally" dropped our *bo*'s, whether full or empty. Or we suddenly had a coughing spell and would have to set the bucket down. Once a note slipped out of my waistband and onto the ground. Knowing I was supposed to bow to every V, no matter how far away, I set my bucket down, turned toward an imaginary Vietnamese, and executed an especially deep bow. While I bent over, I picked up the note. The guard, thinking that I had seen a V, smirked to see me humble myself and did not say a word.

One morning, after I had returned to my cell with three or four notes in my waistband, the guard decided to pull a search. He ordered Kay Russell to put his hands up and proceeded to examine him thoroughly. I was at too close range to move without being obvious. I trembled.

As the guard was about to finish his first examination, I remembered the cliché: the best defense is a good offense. Immediately I walked up to the guard, cowered myself before him, and raised my arms high before he gave the order.

The guard squinted, shrugged his shoulders, pulled out his keys, and shut the door.

I was not always that lucky, however. Because I was so active in passing intelligence, I was bound to get caught. And I was caught, at least a half-dozen times. The common punishment was for guards to force me to my knees and beat me on the face, usually with open hands. I welcomed this punishment because it left only welts and bruises.

I welcomed it because I knew that I would not be victimized by the "fanbelt," a torture technique which I had undergone twice for communicating.

I was caught peeking through a vent to make initial contact with Gary Anderson, whom I'd not seen for several months. Within a minute six guards were inside my cell ordering me out. They took me to an empty room, made me strip completely, and forced me to spread-eagle on the floor with my face down. Four guards stood on my hands and legs. The remaining two guards moved to my sides, carrying eight-foot rubber whips—long belts cut from a tire. They reached behind them as though they were chopping wood and slashed with rapid-fire succession, creating foot-long gashes across my back and buttocks.

I still have the scars.

letters

At my first interrogation I told the V I was not married. I assumed that it would be impossible to communicate with Anne, and I did not want the Vietnamese to bother her by sending harassing reports. The officers assured me that if I observed camp regulations I could write home; they even showed me form letters for that purpose. I felt the V were bribing me to answer more questions, and I wouldn't fall for that trick. A month later I checked with other POWs and found it was in fact possible to write. The mechanics were there and the channels were apparently available, so I decided to tell the Vietnamese officers the truth.

Anne was on my mind day and night. I felt that I was letting her down as a husband, and I was thoroughly frustrated at not being able to fulfill my obligations. My only alternative was to write letters, and I spent many hours composing the messages I would send. I must lift her spirits, to make her know that things would someday be the same and that we'd again enjoy the life we once had. With this in mind, I mentally wrote this poem for her.

> I will take your hand in mine and draw you close to me;
> I will feel your warmth divine and thrill in ecstasy;
> I will close my eyes and thank the Lord that we are free—
>> Not today, not tomorrow, but someday.
>
> You will smile with loving glow as you rush to embrace;
> Your mind will see a flurried snow while searching time and space;
> Your eyes will sparkle and a tender tear will warm your face—
>> Not today, not tomorrow, but someday.

Several months later—on 10 October 1967—the guards directed me to a building we called the Big House and gave me wonderful news: I could write home! I needed no pause to write the words I knew by heart.

Three days later, the guards again led me to the Big House, and officers informed me that my letter needed "some corrections." I could not refer to God or to religion, nor could I list specific dates. The only topics I could discuss were my health, the future, and pro-Vietnamese propaganda. Thus, I was limited to two subjects.

They handed back my letter, half of which was inked out. With only five minutes for a redraft, I almost panicked. The third line of my poem had been censored, and with a guard at my shoulder, I could think of no suitable replacement.

I felt like a student who had found too late a final page to his exam. On the spur of the moment I scribbled: "We will be as happy as two hearts in love can be." I hoped Anne would understand. The censors accepted the new line, but only after three more sessions was the total draft approved.

Returning to my cell was not easy. I had accepted a special favor which my cellmates had not even been offered. When they saw my troubled face, they reassured me, "For goodness sakes, Charlie, if you get a chance to write home, write!" But they had wives, too, and one had children. Why was I the only one selected?

* * *

POWs in our camp heard nothing about sending tapes home until Christmas 1967. Even then, the news was an accident. The voice of Viet Nam inadvertently broadcast the introduction to one of its programs:

Today's broadcast will include taped messages from American prisoners of war to their families.

The V technician immediately silenced the rest of the program, but it was too late. We discovered that a few POWs in another camp had talked to their wives.

The winter of 1967-68 was long, cold, and miserable. On February 2—Groundhog Day—an officer outside our cell hollered at the guard for keys. We broke into a cold sweat. He opened the door and uttered, "Lam, here letter from wife." I bowed, said "Thank you," and extended my hand. The officer dropped it on the bunk.

The envelope had already been opened, and the letter was blemished with smudges and V signatures. Several sentences were inked through. By this time the officer, the guards, and my cellmates gathered around to watch.

Anne wrote that she was in good spirits and was adjusting to her new life. She had planted a garden for my return and had bought carpeting for our home. She sounded very optimistic. I thrilled with exuberance. The beautiful letter was dated 10 July 1967.

I looked up at my cellmates with tears in my eyes. All of our thoughts turned toward home. I now had written a letter and received one, but my buddies had done neither. I confronted the officer, "Why don't these men get mail?" He answered (and we heard the same answer for six years), "If you family write, we give you."

The officer insisted that most families had never written but instead had divorced husbands and disavowed sons to protest this "filthy war." Of course we knew better.

Surprisingly, the officer let me keep the letter. He secured the door, and I had to go to its crack for enough light to memorize one precious line at a time.

I needed to share my good fortune and offered the letter to my cellmates, but all they would take was the envelope. On it were two stamps—one of President Jefferson and the other an airmail stamp of a Boeing 707. We cherished these stamps, tracing and drawing each line for hours. It was amazing how important a common stamp could be after so long a time with no memento from home. I received my second letter about a year later—Christmas, 1968. I was in a different cell, and again none of my buddies received mail. Why only me? I wanted so much for my cellmates to receive news and reassurance, and I pleaded with the officer, "Why? Why?"

"If you family write, we give you."

As before, my cellmates' approach was, "Don't worry about us. Be glad you've got one . . . and we'll look at your stamps."

Inside the letter was a black and white polaroid snapshot. Anne had let her blonde hair grow halfway down her back by then, knowing that I preferred long hair. But I could not see her face. She said nothing about the picture in her letter, and so I was puzzled and disappointed. But I also was very fortunate. I saw the back of my wife's head; my cellmates saw nothing of their wives.

That same week the V ordered a few of us to make tapes. Our SRO had decided that we could record a tape if we felt our wives needed to hear our voices, but most of us decided the tapes were a whitewash of the truth and we would have no part of it.

When the officer commanded that I tape, I flatly refused. Because of my response, I was forced to my knees and hit across the face with fists. It was ironic, but I was determined not to help the V propaganda effort by capitalizing on private opportunities. A strong bond of unity had to be maintained if we POWs were to survive.

One of the prisoners who was particularly concerned about his wife's well-being did make a recording. The V told him that unless he reported his good treatment, the tape would not be broadcast. So, he complied:

Boy, you should have seen the chicken we had for Christmas. It was one B.F.D.—and you know what that means—big fine dinner.

A month after I received the Christmas letter, we heard over the Voice of Viet Nam: "Following the lenient and humane policy of the sovereign nation of the Democratic Republic of Viet Nam, we are going to permit packages to be sent from America to imprisoned war criminals." We jumped through hoops. Our minds danced. We'd have pencils, books, games. Our problems were solved.

During flight training I'd hungered for time to read but never had the chance. Now, all I had was time, and I would finally be able to use it. We speculated on what we would get. Nearly everyone wanted a Bible. Second choices were books of world records, atlases, or almanacs. Third and fourth selections were books containing specific information: how to build a radio, human anatomy, etc. The V told us that the packages would be five kilos—eleven pounds. We could start an extensive library if the books were of onion skin. And plastic playing cards . . . I'd become a champion bridge player!

Our Christmas wish arrived at the end of January 1969. The riddled packages were nearly empty, with only a little candy, a few T-shirts, underpants, and toiletries. The officers had removed all the books and pencils. With them went our dreams.

In my box was one pack of Doublemint chewing gum. I couldn't understand, because my wife knew that I disliked gum.

Conditions improved in the late spring of 1969. As many as fifteen letters for two hundred prisoners were received over a period of four months. Moreover, each letter was top priority material for our comm net. Many of the wives plied word association in their notes, and the result was the stock question: "What do you think she means by this?" Sometimes the message was clear. If a fellow had been promoted, his wife might write, "You are a *major* factor in my plans." or "The tree in our backyard has sprouted silver oak leaves."

Probably the most touching news of all was the announcement of a baby son or daughter to POWs who had left pregnant wives. Not only did the proud father cry, but so did all of us as we tapped the bulletin from room to room. These reminders of new life refreshed our thoughts.

* * *

Prior to spring 1970 some of the fellows still had never received or been allowed to send mail. We could never figure out how the selection was made. It wasn't based on good behavior—some of the fellows who seemed to be camp favorites weren't writing. On the contrary, some of the most defiant men sent letters. They left their leg irons, prepared their messages, and returned again to solitary. We finally surmised that the opportunity to write was given to verified POWs who had been publicized by Vietnamese propaganda.

The V improvised a mass writing plan, and for the first

time *all* POWs were allowed to write home. Many prisoners didn't know if they should use the same address or even if their wives were still alive.

We especially intended to inform families and the Armed Forces in general of the POW numbers and treatment. Ed Hubbard once wrote, "The food is really great here. The only thing which could make it better is a big glass of Alka Seltzer." (In his next package, Ed received what the V thought was candy, and he gulped it down to settle the cabbage soup.) In addition, every man in the cell put his fingerprints on outgoing mail. However, it must have been difficult, if not impossible, to lift these prints because of the duration and the extensive handling by the V.

The increased writing program put a strain on our minds. Now that we could write a letter home every month, what could we say? Our subject matter was still restricted to health and the future. For a challenge, one POW composed a letter utilizing twenty-five song titles. We initiated a contest to see how many words we could write on the seven-line "postcard." I won on several occasions with over 140 words.

More pictures arrived and we noticed that many of the women were wearing silver bracelets. Often these did not match other jewelry; and whether in formal attire or swimsuits, the women had them on. We wondered about these modest bracelets for months. Perhaps some religious group was using them for promotion. Perhaps they were a kind of hula hoop fad.

Not until near the end of the war did we learn the significance of VIVA bracelets. A pilot, just brought into camp, was wearing one! We were astonished. As he walked in we chided: "Hey, look—here's a guy wearing a bracelet! And look at that long hair!"

It was obviously the wrong thing to say. Here we were,

still living in 1967, kidding a man who had come from a world that hadn't stopped. He was nice about it, but he couldn't understand why we were so sarcastic about something so special. Later we understood our mistake and apologized. Engraved on his bracelet was the name of a prisoner in our own camp!

In late 1970 and early 1971, mail started rolling in. We just knew we were going home tomorrow! So much mail was being delivered that we couldn't memorize it all. One happy letter started: "You remember the tree in our backyard that had silver oak leaves? Yesterday it had two eagles sitting in it." Al Runyan had been promoted to bird colonel.

Not all the letters were happy ones, however. Once, the wife of a missing pilot wrote to her husband's RIO saying, "I was driving the car the other day and my dog Smitty [not real name] jumped out and disappeared. Do you know anything about it?" Sadly, he did. Her husband had failed to escape the crash four years earlier. We felt deep respect for this woman who displayed such determination and hope.

The V never made us wait for "Dear Johns." Prisoners who received them handled these letters in various ways. Some went into seclusion and refused to talk to anyone for several days. Others were open, attempting to mask the sad news with strained humor: "Here's the letter, you guys. She's left me—and look out! You'd better lock up your wife and hide your kids!"

One senior officer waited five years before he received his first letter. During that time, it was pitiful to see this proud man drop to his knees and plead with the V: "Just one word from home. Please, just one word. You can scratch everything out but her signature. Just let me know she's still alive. Please!"

"If you family write, we give you."

Finally his day came. He was taken out for mail call. When he returned, we shouted "Congratulations! Terrific!" He walked quietly to his rack, sat down, put his head between his legs, and sobbed for half an hour—but his tears were of joy. He had finally received a letter from home.

After one mail call, a POW returned to his cell from the reading room and recited a line he had memorized: "And Grandma Smith fell down and broke her hip." We tried to comfort him. "I'm sorry to hear that, Jim." "Yeah," he said, "but Grandma Smith has been dead for over ten years." One of the comedians in the corner rebounded a "sick" repartee: "Maybe someone backed over her grave with a truck."

We passed the contents of the letters from one end of the camp to the other, each of us trying to figure word associations or references to unknown people. Did anyone know the redheaded girl who worked in the Safeway supermarket? Negative. Many of the unsolved references related to MIAs or prisoners in other camps.

In 1971 I received several letters from my wife, two from my parents, and two Christmas cards from my sister and brother. I was really in fat city. Not all my mail was being delivered though—some of the letters referred to messages I never received. It was also apparent from Anne's questions that many of my letters had never left the censor's desk.

Once a POW, alone in the room, found a bushel basket filled with letters from the States. He grabbed a couple of them, concealed them under his sleeve, brought them back to the cell, and passed the contents through the walls to their overjoyed owners.

Another time, I forced a desk drawer and saw at least two hundred color photographs from America. One of the first pictures that caught my eye was of two women, probably wife and mother, standing on opposite sides of the American flag. The V had assured us that our families were anti-American, and so this conflicting evidence was, of course, restricted.

I also stole a book which unfortunately contained nothing but anti-American essays. I tied a string to it and eased it through an airspace between the bricked-in window and the exterior wooden shutters. The string broke. With a mirror, I looked down the vent and saw that it rested bottom left. I chewed a stick of gum (which I had saved for several months) until it was soggy, tied it to another string and tried to dive-bomb the book. I missed. I pulled the gum back up, picked off some of the dirt, and chewed it again. I dropped it the second time and scored. A week later I cautiously pulled the string taut. The book was mine.

Packages continued to be delivered to about 75 percent of the prisoners. Each POW was supposed to get them quarterly, but at every delivery the number dropped. Families were not sending fewer packages, but the V were taking more and more of the clothing and food for themselves.

What they didn't want, they pulverized, and the last packages were worthless, often containing nothing more than a half-cup of splintered hard candy or a glob of melted bouillon cubes. These no longer reminded us of home.

* * *

After several years I found that the best method to avert censorship was to insert diversionary messages in the first line: "I received your letter on 20 July 1970" or "Put your trust in God." The censor cut out the obvious infractions, did what he'd been ordered, and generally meddled no further.

Censorship was certainly a problem, but there were factors that bothered us even more. Neither our families nor we could empathize. We were afraid to become personal. If our letters fell into the hands of some anti-war delegation, our intimate thoughts might be splashed across billboards.

At last the time of release approached. In February 1973 I was in the same camp with POW No. 1, my good friend Ev Alvarez. The V had previously given him a newspaper story about his divorce, so he knew he was going home a single man.

Ev was well aware of my love for Anne and offered to carry my mail back to the States while I awaited my freedom. Eight days before he left, I started writing personal thoughts to my wife, knowing that for the first time my letters would be uncensored. I gave three to Ev and the remaining five to other POWs who were among the early releases.

Ev sent the letters as he had promised to do. A few days later he found them unopened in his mailbox. I didn't know it yet, but Anne was no longer interested in my letters . . . or my love.

chain of command

As prisoners of war, we knew full well that we could not withstand the ordeal of imprisonment by ourselves. Our instinct to identify with fellow Americans, our familiarity with the military chain of command and discipline, and our knowledge that we could have strength in numbers motivated us to unify. Alone we had no counsel, no power. Alone we despaired.

My first encounter with military policy occurred three weeks after I was captured. Bob Shumaker, twitching the wire two walls away, notified me that Navy Captain Jim Stockdale, our senior officer in Hanoi Hilton, had initiated military strategy and was releasing directives. My first "twx" (transmission) from Jim was timely guidance: no escape without outside help. Captain Stockdale had scrutinized prison security for nearly two years and concluded that any attempt to escape would be futile without fifth-column help and that such an effort could endanger the lives of remaining POWs.

Bob relayed Captain Stockdale's second and third twx: no work outside camp and no public display. Aid to the enemy must be refused.

At first I was surprised that a chain of command existed in the camp. The structure of our system reflected closely the traditional military hierarchy. Of course, our Navy, Air Force, and Marine Corps were now combined, and initially it was an onerous task to designate senior officers. Some POWs weren't sure of the date they had received their last promotions, and many of us from the academies had made rank simultaneously. Had we been free, we could have checked our lineal numbers in the *Blue Book* to settle the controversy; but since we did not have access to it we agreed to assign seniority in these cases by alphabetical order of last names.

Naturally none of us expected promotions while we were in prison. Stateside, we would have been promoted one, and perhaps two, ranks. Younger men were shot down four or five years later, entering the prison with less time but with higher rank. As a consequence, these less qualified men took command. (In actuality, however, they were still lower in rank because we had been given promotions in absentia.)

Obviously, a revision was necessary. To ascertain seniority with someone imprisoned years later, I referred to my rank on 19 May 1967 and compared his time and grade on that same date. In the summer of 1972, an Annapolis classmate Ted Triebel was shot down as a lieutenant commander, two promotions higher than my rank as a lieutenant, junior grade. Since our time and grade were no different on 19 May 1967, we applied the alphabet and he played "plebe."

In each camp was an SRO (Senior Residing Officer) in charge of 50 to 360 men, depending on the camp and year.

Under him were Building SROs, with a charge of about twenty men. Down the chain were Room SROs, with two or three men.

Taking command was not simple. The V usually found out who was in charge and frequently tortured him. Some men were so brutally beaten or had spent so much time in solitary confinement that they were reluctant to chance further reprisal by involving themselves with such clandestine activities.

In one case, Camp Plantation officials received two American officers who were really torn up. Multiple scars showed that bamboo stakes had impaled their feet, and their macabre bodies seemed close to starvation. Understandably, these men shook from fear when approached by guards. Nonetheless, they were our most qualified senior officers.

Some of us took terrifying risks to open communications with these men. If they left clothing on the line, we clipped notes inside a shirt-sleeve. If they went out to bathe or to dump their *bo*'s, we shouted, "Name! Name!" They immediately turned away. They followed camp regulations explicitly. Although we tried everything we could imagine to make contact, it was no use. We were frustrated to risk our safety only to be shunned.

One day, as the two men showered in the six-by-six-foot cubicle, one of us in an adjacent stall shouted into a drain pipe at the floor. The noise erupted inside their stall, alerting the guard. He warned them to keep quiet or be punished. We shouted again, and again the guard threatened. The men knew that the only way to keep us quiet and to avoid unjust punishment was to answer back. They did, and communications began. These senior officers were soon grateful that we had forced them into the comm system. They took charge with enthusiasm and competence.

Making sure that everyone was on our team was the first of many objectives. Understanding the rules of the game was the second. It was assumed that all of us had a basic knowledge of military discipline and the Code of Conduct. This code—a very general document—was open to many interpretations. How we construed the code often depended on the severity of the situation. No longer could we pick up a telephone and call the Pentagon for advice.

The broad spectrum of the code divided the men into at least two groups: those who were disciplinarians by nature and interpretated the Code strictly, and those who were liberal and rendered the Code loosely. We called these groups the "Tough Guys" and the "Softies."

"Softy" was not derogatory. The name simply indicated a different approach to the Code. Tough Guys who referred to the line "I will never surrender of my own free will," sometimes flaunted their incorrigibility and taunted the guards. The Vietnamese answered with torture, and the Tough Guys occasionally relinquished more information than the Softies who never committed themselves.

Regardless of our attitudes we were all in the same boat. Each of us had acquiesced to V control to some extent, whether accepting cigarettes or bowing to guards. The line which separated the Tough Guys from the Softies was often unclear. The important thing was to display unity, regardless of our individual philosophies. We clearly understood that the V would capitalize on any chinks they found in our armor.

Unity didn't evolve automatically. Learning its value required from us much introspection and sacrifice. How could a Camp SRO appease the Softies if he interpreted the Code "too strictly"? Or if he was too lax for the Tough Guys? He was in an untenable position, having little control over the actions of men in other rooms. He had excessive responsibility but none of the tools of authority—reduction of salary, suspension of liberty, court-martial. Indeed, most of the fellows he had never seen, his only association being a tap on the wall or a scribbled message.

Even against the enemy, he had no weapons to reinforce his position. On the contrary, he made great efforts to conceal the fact that he was calling the shots. Otherwise, the Vietnamese would put him in isolation or take him to another camp.

To meet this impractical setting, the SROs wielded gentle sticks of diplomacy. They knew we were not "boots" who asked "How high?" at the command to jump. We were all trained leaders who acted independently. For the first few years, the SRO's authority was limited to advice rather than orders. Realizing the importance of unity, we respected this advice as though it were an order.

A serious problem existed within the communications network itself. Relaying an order was a vulnerable game of password. We never knew what form the message would take as it was tapped to the opposite end of the camp. Sometimes, messages in transit had to be delayed for weeks, and comm teams could not always remember the exact wording.

Even if we had passed the message verbatim, we still questioned its legality. What if we refused an order on the basis that it did not come from the commander but rather from five men who interpreted it through an error-ridden system? What if compliance to the order brought certain torture? We were very alone in answering these questions.

Once I received the order "Plumb, request you communicate with Captain Abbott at all costs." What did the SRO mean by "at all costs"? Did it include being caught and put in leg irons for months at a time?

Frequently the camp would be in a comm purge which continued until tortured prisoners identified the comm teams (of which I was always a member). When this occurred the commander directed: "Suspend all nonessential communication." Was the recipe for Mom's apple pie nonessential? To me this type of message was important because it was our vital morale builder. I'm sure that I didn't always interpret the orders the way my commander intended. But I, as all of us, used my best judgment and trusted my comrades' decisions up the chain as well as down.

Although the Son Tay raid in late 1970 rescued no prisoners, it offered some valuable consolations. We were all joined together inside one perimeter wall. Fortunately, our senior men were housed in the same general area, and immediately they went to work designing effective POW regulations. These detailed interpretations of the Code of Conduct became known as the "plums," the product of great foresight and leadership ability. (I don't know who invented that term, but many fellows chided me, thinking I was the ghost writer.)

Approximately 260 POWs became organized into the Fourth Allied POW Wing. We were divided into squadrons, flights, and sections. Each subdivision with its own commander attained the same pride we had once known in our flying units. Now we could act as one body—mates in one cell wouldn't be on a hunger strike while fellows in the next cell ate cookies. We had bargaining power.

The first items in the plums were our release and post-release procedures. As early as 1970 we decided to say nothing about our treatment until all the men were home. We insisted that the order of release would be first the sick and injured, then the enlisted, and finally officers in order of longest imprisonment.

Another plum stated the appropriate POW conduct with the Vietnamese. We would by no means aid the V in whitewashing the truth about our conditions. At the same time we would be considerate to the V in hopes of improved treatment.

One of the plums described procedures for resistance conditions (res cons). Res Con No. 6 was simply our military bearing with the enemy—to offer consideration to them, but with disdain. Intermediate res cons were the refusal to stand or talk when the V came to the door, or the refusal to keep quiet after the evening gong sounded. Res con No. 1, our last condition, was a hunger strike. We were normally under res con No. 6 and once resorted to res con No. 1, bargaining successfully for the rights to sing and to have worship. (None of the res cons were violent: we had no plans to riot or destroy prison facilities.)

In each room several men (called the Memory Bank) memorized every plum to keep the regs consistent. The plums were long—several at least ten paragraphs—but they were concisely written and outlined. (I was a member of the communications team, often its chief officer, who cross-checked the accuracy of the memory banks. Since the plums were very specific, with times and dates and particular conduct in a variety of situations, communication was especially difficult. Many times our system had no punctuation. Plums dealing with the communication system itself were highly classified, and unscrambling these codes was tedious business.)

Memory Banks also filed in their minds the names, ranks, and order of shoot-down of every prisoner. They helped the comm team identify call signs (code names of officers): "Jingo to Diamond" or "Salty [a Navy man] to Mule [Westpoint grad]." Often SROs used the same flight call signs they had used when they were shot down. (Had my squadron commander been captured, he would probably have designated himself as "Lindfield.") One of my SROs, who had an eye put out when he was captured, was "Cyclops."

SROs now had a unified force to confront the enemy. They also had authority to control the behavior of prisoners. A less severe punitive measure was a note of reprimand: "I think you are about to violate the Code of Conduct. I recommend that you refuse to make a tape." The most severe action was the suspension of one's military authority.

The important questions remained unresolved: Were the plums really binding by military law? How would a man withstand court martial proceedings if he disobeyed? Were the squadron commanders exerting more control than they rightfully possessed? None of us knew for certain. Personally, I felt that the plums were a unifying influence and that it made little difference who called the signals as long as we all ran toward the same goal.

But the goal posts were opposite. The direction had to be certain. One plum stated: "You will accept no favors from the enemy, and you will attempt to get improved treatment for everyone." To identify the goal post, the commander assigned an RTF (reasonable time frame) whenever a POW was given a favor. For instance, the V gave my room a pencil. For us, this was Christmas five times over. The commander prescribed, "Your RTF is one month." Unless all the rooms received a pencil within the month, we were to give it back to the V. We did, but it wasn't easy.

Mature, professional soldiers felt that in some cases they were not bound to the plums. On Christmas 1971 the V offered to let some men write letters, prepare tapes, and send pictures home. Obviously, the V were not going to broadcast 350 tapes or take 350 snapshots.

Since everyone could not participate, the SRO judged the acceptance of this favor "unlawful." Three POWs disagreed, justifying their argument by saying the tapes were of minimum propaganda value and of maximum benefit to their families. They made tapes. For that action the SRO relieved these men of their rank for ninety days. (Another man wanted very much to make a tape because his wife had encountered a series of mishaps and had suffered a mental breakdown. He appealed, and his commander gave him permission.)

Toward the end of the war, our senior men were in a strong enough position to request an interview with the enemy camp commander. Months later the request was granted. Our officers reported, "We need medical attention for specific individuals. If we don't receive it, we will refuse to stand before your guards and will not carry out our *bo*'s."

The increasing strength from unity made impact and our demands were met.

POWs were often forced to interpret plums on the spot. If V officers entered our room and said, "You-you-you, put on long clothes, roll up blanket, and step out here," we had to decide whether to resist or to comply. Often, the SRO was near the door to give hand gestures or to nod. While he signaled, another prisoner distracted the officer by complaining about a hole in his cup or feigning a dizzy spell.

Once a V officer demanded that two of our men leave the room to make coal balls. The SRO's signal: No. The prisoners, refusing to obey the V order, were taken out and for one month were chained to the same leg irons. (Although the V didn't know it, these two men had fought cat-and-dog and had stayed at opposite corners of our cell.) They learned to get along together. They had to.

To frustrate our chain of command, the V attempted a

counter-measure. Instead of allowing us our own senior officer, *they* picked the man—usually a junior officer whom they named "Chief" or "Head."

At first we didn't know how to handle this, but we soon initiated a JOL (junior officer liaison) program. I had been selected "Chief," and whenever the V called me out for instructions, I replied, "I can't order these men to do anything. They have higher rank. How can I tell them to keep quiet?"

But when it was time to accept a favor, such as a pencil, I took it; and when the officer left, I gave it to my SRO. Because of our JOL setup we were able to appease the V and at the same time maintain our own command.

If a senior officer wanted to pull rank on his men he did. Most of the senior men, however, carried out honey buckets and swept floors with the rest of us. All of us knew that when things got tough, he was going to earn those few privileges he had.

Only three enlisted men were in our camp—Air Force medics and a Marine sergeant. These fine soldiers insisted on doing more than their share of the dirty work. We knew that this kind of subservience was not applicable in our situation, so we gave them officer training and temporary battlefield commissions. (Since their return two of the men have become officers. The third was deathly ill when the V took him from our camp. He didn't return to the States.)

The development of our command chain was out of necessity. It was only our close unity which allowed us to (1) deny the V propaganda and comfort; (2) improve on living conditions; (3) keep morale high; and (4) return home with honor.

Because of the wise leadership of our commanding officers these goals were reached.

exercises

What was it like to exist within the confines of dark vermin-infested walls? After a month, after a year, after six years, those walls never offered security; not once during my imprisonment did I sleep undisturbed from gong to gong.

After my capture, I discovered that my fear of being brainwashed was unfounded. My need to downshift from a Phantom catapult to a numbing catalepsy was not. A feeble bulb superseded an instrument panel. Tedium choked exhilaration. Loneliness jettisoned camaraderie. The hare became the tortoise.

My body ached, and I lay day after day not wanting to move. I knew that I must escape the patient Vietnamese trap set to atrophy my mind and body. But I hurt. My back and my thigh hurt. My cellmate Kay Russell hurt too.

Days passed. My body yearned for activity. Very slowly, I tried a sit-up. After a half hour of agony, I completed my maneuver until my fingers touched my knees. I wrenched my

hands and stretched my toes. Pus exuded from the ulcerated bayonet wound. I cried.

But I could not let myself quit and within two months I accomplished my first real sit-up. A few weeks later both Kay and I were able to force twenty-five push-ups and seventy-five sit-ups. Our beds in the center, we jogged circles around the room until we reached a mile each day.

We applied all kinds of isometrics, pushing one fist against the other or trying to pull apart hands clasped behind our necks. We twisted rags into a stretching machine and pulled one arm against the other. Our beds—six-pound wooden pallets—became weights and Kay and I curled them in unison for coordination.

As time progressed and our comm net improved, I learned still more ways to exercise. One method was what POWs called an inverto, a handstand push-up with feet against the wall. Several of the guys could do twenty of them, and when they finished their eyes looked like road maps. If rooms had beds on stanchions, we stepped up and down, employing an exercise similar to the Harvard Step Test. And if the room was too small for us to move about freely, we simply ran in place.

Challenges from one room to another became popular: "How many push-ups and sit-ups can you do?" Our record graduated slowly, first at twenty-seven and a week later twenty-eight. Someone reached thirty-four, and the challengers struggled to make thirty-five. By the time I was released, the push-up record peaked at 1500 and the sit-up challenge was over 10,000!

The most impressive challenge came from Barry Bridger. Barry stood unsupported on his hands, lowered himself until his nose touched the floor, and muscled himself back to straightened arms . . . twenty-seven times! Most of us couldn't do any, and we had flat noses from trying.

We learned to juggle. Using wadded rags, we tossed three, four, sometimes five makeshift balls. Some of the fellows developed new tricks throwing balls to each other. We stripped rags into quarter-inch pieces and used lanyard braid to make jump ropes, and when we couldn't hide them we passed the ropes off as strings to tie up our mosquito nets. Like agile boxers, forty-year-old men crossed their wrists and whipped the rope around twice at each jump.

Many thought their exercising would build muscles. That wasn't the case. One cellmate exercised four hours a day, six days a week for three years. He increased his stunts but not his measurements; his biceps, thighs, and calves measured exactly the same as when he went in. He had the time and the routine, but he simply didn't have the fuel. Our low-protein meals were not building blocks, nor were we "spring chickens." Some of the men thought their muscle size was increasing, but in reality they were only losing fat and seeing more muscle definition.

Each POW had his own idea of the physical training best suited for him. Some wanted bulk and lifted buckets, while others strained a little each day just to keep their hearts pumping. A few exercised to keep their tennis serve, golf swing, or ski slalom. In 1968 our SRO advised us to do a minimum of fifty push-ups and one hundred sit-ups a day. We were going to go home in good shape in spite of Vietnamese ideas to the contrary. As a matter of fact, the Vietnamese, seeing us become stronger, decided that exercise was against camp regulations, and from time to time they forbade it altogether. Daily enforcement of this restriction seemed to depend on how much sleep the V commander got the night before. Physical exercise was difficult, but our bodies were quick to adapt.

It took me longer to realize that my mind collected cobwebs too. No automatic sensors informed me of this as had been the case with my body. The first activity I undertook was the effort to recall every incident in my life. I tried to envision every course I had ever taken at school, every movie I'd seen, every birthday, every person I'd met. Nine hundred hours later, I reached the last pages of my life story. When I did have a new recollection, I designated it as a virgin thought. By 1969 I had no more than one original thought a month, and I replaced these worn-out records with day-to-day experiences. This is the chief reason I can remember so many details of my imprisonment.

I exchanged my life story for my cellmate's. Kay Russell and I discussed every song, every television program, every sport, the war, history, geography, religious doctrines, philosophies, everything, until there was almost nothing original left for us to share. At that point, our minds were scraped clean, and silence saturated the room for hours at a time. Our only diversions became clinking keys or plodding oxen.

We tried to develop our own "academics." We practiced imaginary pianos and guitars. We spent much time memorizing Bible verses. We also studied lists, the most important of which was names of all the POWs. When we got out, these lists would be very important. Some of the men memorized the names alphabetically. Some categorized the POWs by shootdown date. Some listed the men by camp, building, and room. Some did all three. My latest list contained about 360 names, and each morning I rattled it off in about five minutes. I had said the names so often that it was easy to remember a fellow POW when we met for the first time after our release: "Oh, yeah. Newcomb. You came between Neuens and Nix."

Next I memorized names of all the American and English authors I could summon. I also recited a list of sixty-five aircraft manufacturers and each of the ten or fifteen varieties of planes they had built. One sports enthusiast, Galand Kramer, memorized the names of over 750 baseball players, and after that list became tiresome he memorized it in reverse.

Groups of POWs formed into the Punsters and the Anti-punsters. The Anti-punsters did not appreciate puns and refused to laugh at them. The Punsters, always trying to get into the knickers of the Anti-punsters, sneaked around and fished them into a pun when they least expected it. Some punsters became very adept, having repartee for every occasion.

We played games. One was called "Ghost," and each man was supposed to add another letter to a word he was building and pass it to the next POW. One fellow would say a.n.t.h.r.o.p.o.m.o . . . and the next would continue a.n.t. h.r.o.p.o.m.o.r. Those of us who weren't in the game let our minds wander, but we were thinking about the word too. We waited twenty, twenty-five, thirty-five minutes for Bob to add the next letter, but we heard nothing. We looked over. Bob was sound asleep. From that day on, whenever Bob went to bed, we whispered to the others: "He's playing Ghost."

One fellow in my building, Norm Wells, had a wonderful gift. When he was a young boy, his parents asked him to memorize a poem every year to recite at their Thanksgiving reunions. These poems weren't the "Mary Had a Little Lamb" kind, either, but rather long poems such as Kipling's "The Battle of East and West" and "Gunga Din" and Noyes' "The Highwayman."

Since we had no safe way of copying the verses down and keeping them, Norm passed one verse a day through the walls for us to memorize. This was really challenging. I still remember the forty-five stanzas before the Colonel's son and Kamal's boy rode the mare and the dun "back to Fort Bukloh where there went forth but one." As we memorized "The Highwayman," the prisoners next door had to move out just as Bess was about to "shatter her breast in the moonlight" in order to warn the Highwayman that the Red Coats had besieged the inn. So that our departing poetry lovers wouldn't leave in suspense, we smuggled a tiny note telling the outcome: "The Highwayman and Bess—K.I.A."

The poems were not only entertaining but also meaningful. I remember vividly the night I first heard and memorized William Ernest Henley's "Invictus," which represented so well our circumstances and our feelings:

> Out of the night that covers me,
>   Black as the Pit from pole to pole,
> I thank whatever gods may be
>   For my unconquerable soul.
>
> In the fell clutch of circumstance
>   I have not winced nor cried aloud.
> Under the bludgeonings of chance
>   My head is bloody, but unbowed.
>
> Beyond this place of wrath and tears
>   Looms but the horror of the shade,
> And yet the menace of the years
>   Finds, and shall find, me unafraid.
>
> It matters not how strait the gate,
>   How charged with punishments the scroll,
> I am the master of my fate;
>   I am the captain of my soul.

idiosyncrasies

"Hey, fellah. You sprayed your germs all over my soup!"

"What the heck, man. My hands were full."

"Yeah. Full of *my* contaminated soup!"

"Well, if you don't like it, carry your own."

We lived on top of each other, and none of us liked where we lived. We had problems which never would have occurred under normal circumstances. Our sensitivity increased, our discretion clouded, and patience often disappeared. Absurdly simple things grated on our nerves and soured our dispositions.

How could we tell someone that his snorts or grinding of teeth while he slept drove us up a wall? What good would it do to say anything at all? The solution was simply that each of us had to learn to overcome our peeves. We were an extremely proud group of men and would be humiliated to admit that we could be bothered by some petty idiosyncrasy. We told ourselves that if we weren't mature enough to adjust to personality conflicts and irksome mannerisms, we were the ones in error.

Still, it was easier to say than to feel. In six years, half a dozen incidents bothered me so that I could no longer grin and bear it. For a solution I approached a third party and, as tactfully as I could, said, "Hey, can you help me out? I know it's my fault, and I'm trying to overcome it, but I just can't get used to the stench from the bucket. Sometimes old Scatterbrain forgets to put the lid back after he's finished. Would you say something to him about it? I'll keep trying to adjust, but right now I almost throw up." This approach was usually successful.

In eight-by-eight-foot rooms, we couldn't run. In the larger rooms, the guys who had irrevocable conflicts moved to opposite corners and avoided each other. On only two or three occasions did they resort to fisticuffs.

* * *

Moving in with a new cellmate was like walking into the Smithsonian for the first time. He was a brand-new source of information and entertainment, and we would sit up the first night discussing every topic we could imagine. But after three months, we had exhausted all common interest, and as predictable as the seven-year-itch, conversations crumbled to arguments.

One very controversial issue was cigarette smoking. Nonsmokers saw no reason to step on ashes or to jeopardize health by inhaling trapped smoke. But for smokers, a cigarette was the highlight of the day. They waited for it, they craved it, and when they got it, they were content to the last draw.

Smokers cultivated particular mannerisms for this special occasion. Some guys found the cigarette so relaxing that they withdrew from everything and everyone and became recluses for five minutes. They wanted silence. Others liked to talk when they smoked. Some liked to sit on the bucket, and at times we didn't have enough *bo*'s to go around.

Although some took little puffs, others super-inhaled and at the last moment sucked in a quick breath to capture maximum nicotine.

Vietnamese tobacco was of ragweed quality. Often a fellow, taking a puff, would find that his cigarette had gone out. He'd look at the end of it to discover a dried cockroach, a stick, a rock, or a wad of paper. To keep this from happening again, he would roll each cigarette between his hands to dislodge any foreign objects.

The cigarettes often contained holes, and it was necessary for the smoker to make a patch by pasting toilet paper and rice glue around the hole. If he had no patch, he kept the cigarette lit by holding his finger over the hole. If there were several holes he would handle it like a piccolo.

Of course, the smokers burned the cigarettes down to the nub. If one didn't smoke to the finger-burns, another picked up the butt, smoked it down to a quarter inch, and threw the few remaining strands into a pile. Whenever the butt pile contained enough tobacco to make a cigarette or two, the smokers would gather like witches around their brew, strip off the paper, and sort the tar-blackened tobacco.

Finding paper for homemade cigs was not easy. Toilet paper was too porous and, except in a real pinch, was out of the question. Some guys tore off blank corners of their wives' precious letters.

Several smokers were afraid of lung cancer and devised their own filters. Wads of toilet paper, rags, and pieces of straw or bamboo were shoved into the end. This "purified" smoke comforted them, especially when they showed the gummy filter to the mainliners.

Just as our pumpkin soup, these camel-dung cigarettes were of various degrees of mediocrity. Some were weak, some strong. All of them were hot, and none burned long. No smoker could set his cig down and expect it to stay lit for more than twenty or thirty seconds, depending on the humidity. It was therefore important that smokers keep their cigs dry. At first all they had was toilet paper or a little bag made of rags. After packages came in, however, everybody had plastic—and the problem of wet cigarettes was solved . . . until the V took all the plastic.

Until 1970 we couldn't burn homemade punks of rolled toilet paper. Smokers smoked when the guards gave them a light, which was not often. A guy who could steal a box of matches during his interrogation was really king because he could have a cigarette whenever he wanted, or he could even smoke half and save the rest for later. I had once read how prisoners slit matches into four pieces with a razor blade, making four lights instead of one. I wasn't a smoker and didn't need the matches; but the other guys did so I quartered a match to make it go further. Unfortunately for me and the smokers, none of them would ignite.

Some of the smokers worked year after year trying to develop a method to make fire without matches. Of course, we knew the jungle survival methods—rubbing sticks together or using flint and steel—but as far as I know they never succeeded in getting one started.

The smokers did learn how to make a flame from embers, however. There were times when all they had was a glowing cigarette. They would roll up a piece of toilet paper, singe one end with the ember, then unroll the paper very slowly so that the spark would cover a wider area. At the same time they puffed hard and fast through the paper cylinder. This would take as long as five minutes and fill the room with smoke, but eventually the paper would burst into flame. The nonsmokers would burst into cheers.

As the months wore on, many of the smokers—particularly those who felt they were going home in just a few more days—became concerned about the dark brown stains on their fingers and the burns on their lips. We could always recognize the optimist: the guy with the cigarette holder. Men discovered early that the toothpick used by the bum in the comic strips didn't work at all. To solve that, they sandwiched the cigarette between little sticks of a bamboo tweezer. Some found small chunks of mahogany, and with a nail and the concrete floor patiently ground the wood down into holders. Other smokers used pieces of tin, toothpaste tubes, bread, rice dough, or clay.

Cigarette ashes were also causes of friction. Nonsmokers didn't want ashes all over their clothing and beds, yet it was impossible for smokers to keep ashes to themselves. Some smokers made ashtrays by soaking bread in water and pressing the dough. Ashtrays were also made from clay, toilet paper and rice glue, hollowed wood, or an orange peel. The usual tray, however, was the floor.

* * *

A source of continual amusement, and at times problems, was the *bo*—the Vietnamese word for glass, pitcher, bucket, and what we had thought they were trying to say—bowl.

My first *bo* was a rusted out funnel-shaped container with no lid or handle. When I emptied it, I had to carry it with one hand on either side—leaving no hand to hold my nose. I tried to devise lids from toilet paper to arrest the odor, but they didn't work.

After two months, the V brought in a better bucket—a two-gallon container with lid—and white porcelain bowls resembling potties.

Fortunately, the lids ameliorated most of the stench. I and many of the other POWs developed a tremendous sensitivity to odor. In the dead air of a cell where smoke ascended undisturbed, a cellmate would lift the bucket lid fourteen feet away, and within seconds I could discern the odor. I tried my best to be blasé, especially during meals, but I never became accustomed to an open *bo*.

Of course we had no porcelain seat to sit on, and the rim of the bucket was uncomfortable. Some guys used what we called the cantilever method, holding themselves a few inches above the *bo*. The one drawback to this method was that it caused a splash factor of 7 or 8 . . . and some were left in worse shape than if they had sat down. To solve this problem, many would put a layer of toilet paper over the top of the liquid, reducing the splash factor to about 0.5.

One night when Hanoi had a power failure a fellow of the cantilever syndrome was perched above the bucket. His cellmate commented, "I didn't hear anything."

"I didn't either," he admitted. "I forgot to take the lid off."

We could always tell who used the cantilever method because when he stood up he was generally unblemished. But for sitters, it was different. They would return with perfect twelve-inch bucket imprints around their "cheeks."

Some ingenious fellow took pains to balance his sandals on either side of the bucket; he could sit on them and relax in comfort. When he got up, however, he was branded with bright-red footprints.

Just before I moved out of the Plantation to another camp, guards discovered and reclaimed a fountain pen which I had stolen and concealed. I was very unhappy to have lost the pen, and of course I wanted another one. During my first day at the Zoo, I was led to the interrogation room and saw a pen on the officer's desk. When the questioner turned I grabbed it compulsively and hid it under my sleeve. Back in my room I showed the pen to my cellmates, and we decided to call up the guys next door to tell them what I had done. When they heard, they sent back frantic messages stating that the camp was in the middle of a purge: "You're in deep trouble. You'll be strung up by the thumbs."

To make matters worse, I had stolen the pen from an officer we called J.C., who acted as though he were the perfect officer—the meanest, ugliest torturer in the camp.

"What should I do?" I tapped.

"I don't know, but you'd better get rid of it someway." My neighbors were "old heads" and should have known what they were talking about, but they were so engrained with the thought that stealing was a capital offense that they never dared the risk themselves.

Where could I hide the pen? At the Plantation guards never looked in the bucket. I unscrewed the barrel, separated all the pieces, and threw in the whole thing.

I called the guys back: "I've put it someplace they'll never look—the bucket."

"What have you done! That's the first place they go in this camp. You'd better get it out of there!"

I left the wall, rolled up my sleeve, fished out the parts and put the pen back together. I remembered the crawl hole covered with barbed wire in the ceiling fourteen feet above. I stood back, took several aims, and finally I hit the target. That was the end of my pen.

The next day guards escorted my senior officer Mike McCuistion out of our cell. This meant they were going to get tough. They came in several times to search for the pen; and when they couldn't find it, they slapped me around.

The day following, Mike was taken out again, and my

cellmate Bob Wideman and I were moved to an adjacent room. We peeked out a crack and saw that a guard entered our cell with a ladder. This is it, we thought. Mike has been tortured and he's told them where the pen was. Shortly thereafter, another guard came along with a roll of electrical wire. We cringed, unable to prepare ourselves for another "rope trick."

Seconds turned to minutes. What were they doing? A half hour later, guards opened our door and led us back to our room. They had wired in a new propaganda speaker.

Except for clumsy bed pallets, the buckets were our only weights for morning exercise and fellows used buckets for curls and toe-lifts. One day, after twenty-two hours of use, the bucket was filled close to the brim and, as we should have expected, there was too much strain for the handle. Kersplosh! Since it was against regulations to exercise, we quickly grabbed our clothes and sopped up the floor. The guard on duty that day was a guy we named "Magoo" because he squinted his eyes and had difficulty seeing. As bad as he reeked the stench of the room was so much worse that he didn't come in. All of us headed for the bucket, wanting to get outside. The room stunk for several days and unfortunately cleared our sinuses.

* * *

POW sleeping habits varied widely. Our beds of concrete or warped boards were covered with rice mats too thin to provide comfort. Some of the fellows couldn't sleep on their stomachs; some couldn't sleep on their backs. A few tried to bolster some part of their bodies by rolling rags underneath their waists. After several months of lying on my side, I had forced my spine to curve so that my entire body was flush to the mat, even though I was very thin. One of the prisoners had a deviated septum and couldn't get enough air through his nose. Yet it really bothered him to sleep with his mouth open. He solved the dilemma by sleeping all night with one finger propping his nostril open.

Summers were so hot that when I lay on my back, perspiration pooled in my eye sockets and the salinity burned my eyes. I couldn't sleep on my side because I had too much skin on skin, the cause of severe rashes, so I had to learn how to sleep spread-eagle on my stomach.

We lay on the concrete racks fanning ourselves with pieces of cardboard or the lid from a potty. I have often seen prisoners fall asleep while fanning themselves. They would drop their fans but their hands would keep on moving back and forth, back and forth for at least five minutes. I, too, have awakened to see my hand pumping involuntarily.

In the winter the temperature often reached 35° to 40° F. We knew we'd never get warm, but we did want to keep from freezing. Each of us had two blankets, and the question was how to put them to best use. Some fellows wrapped the width of one blanket from their waist down like a serape, and the other was wrapped waist up. They tied the ends of the blankets to close their cocoons. Others would strip down and place their clothing between the blankets (sandwich-style) to create a pocket of air for insulation.

From 1967 to 1970 we were not allowed to stay in our cocoons during the day. Of course, we had no socks or gloves or even handkerchiefs, and the winters were really grim. I usually wrapped my shirt around my head, put my hands under my armpits, and folded my legs Indian style so that each foot was at the inside of the opposite knee. We were required to keep our blankets and extra clothing neatly folded on the bed; but when we could get by with it, we threw the blankets over our heads and, like camouflaged lions, paced back and forth the entire day.

Exercising while someone was asleep was a cause for friction. It may have seemed inconsiderate for cellmates to talk and pace while others tried to sleep, but some of the prisoners wanted to sleep twenty hours a day. During the last few years, the SROs established a policy which stated, "Noise starts at the 6:30 gong and ends at the 12:00 o'clock gong. After siesta, noise will commence at 2:00 o'clock and end at the 9:00 o'clock gong. We will sleep when the V sleep. If you want to make noise, you will wait until the noise periods." The policy solved the issue.

Snoring was a particular problem because it was obviously uncontrollable. At the Plantation I slept in the middle of a cell with Bob Wideman on one side and Mike McCuistion on the other. Bob was a tremendous snorer, and Mike was unable to sleep, but he didn't want to crawl out of his warm cocoon either. He often reached down, picked up one of his sandals and flung it at Bob. More often than not, he hit him. We got into trouble several times because the snoring was so loud that the guards accused us of communicating.

Most of us were given to pacing: it was exercise, and—more important—it was something to do. There were fast pacers and slow pacers. Some dragged their sandals, and some wore no shoes at all. All these things were potentially irritating. In many of the rooms, our bunks were simply another floor level, and guys didn't appreciate pacers walking on their bunks with dirty feet. We had to set up rules to cover that, too.

Personal idiosyncrasies were easy to spot during mealtime. Several of the prisoners were very finicky, tossing out anything that was charred or didn't look quite right. Some fixed their food in various ways each day, mashing the rice and putting it in their pumpkin soup or drinking the broth and spreading the remaining chunks on the rice to make a casserole. Prior to 1969 prisoners ground peanuts and put them into their rice or pumpkin soup, or mixed the whole concoction together. Then the Russians found that they could refine the peanuts into fuel and contracted to buy all of them from North Viet Nam. That was the end of the peanut swill, so fellows tried to make pumpkin pie by mashing up the lumps and spreading it on wet bread. It never tasted like Mom's.

Some of us liked to save things. I think this stemmed from a psychological urge to own something of value. Food was about all we had, but it was tough to save because of the rats, mice, and bugs. We couldn't trust our cups with "airtight" lids. Once I put a piece of bread in my cup and the next morning lifted the lid to see a fat cockroach an inch and a quarter long. How it got there, I'll never know.

Because our last meal was only four hours after the first, we were left with a twenty-hour empty stomach. To remedy that, prisoners pressed rice into balls and wrapped them in a rag until evening snack time. Some POWs ate rice a grain at a time just to pass the day.

Prisoners had varying degrees of sensitivity about the handling of their food. Some were very concerned that other POWs might sneeze or stick thumbs into the soup. This supersensitivity necessitated still another policy: "Everyone will bring in his own soup."

When we dished our food, we were very careful to ladle equitable servings. However, guards usually dipped our soup, and they never cared about portions. My cellmates agreed to rotate daily the first spot in the chow line. Ed Hubbard won the toss and started the evolution. The first day he took the thinnest broth instead of the best. The next day, Larry Spencer did the same. We all followed suit and not a word had to be said.

Several prisoners were enthusiastic tailors. They made needles by filing down wire and drilling the eye with a sharpened piece of tin. At times, they spent months fashioning their tools, only to pop the eye at the last minute. Then they started again, and if they were successful, they would pull thread from shirts or blankets to start their projects. Hands were kept busy as they embroidered designs—an anchor or initials. Ed Mechenbier embroidered a picture of his wife. Mike Christian designed an American flag on the back of his shirt; for this effort, guards took him to the courtyard and beat him severely.

* * *

The V seldom bathed and saw no reason why we should. We kept asking for baths, and finally in 1970 we were allowed to bathe daily. In the winter, bathing was of course difficult because we had nothing but ice-cold water. Some of the men didn't seem to mind, however, and they splashed and splashed. Others bathed no more than once a month, using the philosophy: "I never heard of a guy dying from B.O. and I'm not about to get pneumonia."

One very cold winter, the V camp commander came to us with regulations for taking a bath. At first we laughed.

"What does he know about baths? He got his sweet smell from perfume. We've been bathing for thirty years." We'd been bathing for thirty years all right, but not in ice-cold water . . . and so we listened:

"Exercise before you take bath. Start low on body and wash up very slowly. Wet feet, then knees, then legs, until you get chest area. No direct dousing."

We discovered that the guy knew what he was talking about.

The V required prisoners to shave, at first once every two weeks and later twice a week. We lathered with lye soap and shared one blade among three or four fellows. Using a double-edge, that meant two guys to a side. The question was, should the guy with the heavy beard shave first because he was the toughest to shave? Or should the guy with a light beard shave first because he wouldn't dull the blade?

When we had no mirrors, we shaved by braille. If our shaves failed to pass inspection, a roommate had to play barber. This happened quite frequently when tortured prisoners lost sensitivity in their hands. Some POWs shaved their armpits and crotches in the summer to avoid rash and odor. Of course, they suffered when the bristles grew out.

One fellow was tortured by the V to "show his face" in front of an important delegation. The V officers, wanting to impress the visitors, told him to bathe and shave. Inside the bath cubicle, the prisoner mowed a two-inch strip across the top of his head and came out smiling. This audacious protest embarrassed and angered the V officers. They could no longer put him on display. To teach us all a lesson, the guards beat him in the courtyard so that we would hear his screams.

* * *

I have never seen anything like the pink eye epidemic. We knew it was coming, but we didn't know what to do about it. Two hundred and fifty men lived in nine cells, and in a matter of three hours, the epidemic completely encompassed a room. Someone's eyes swelled and watered, and soon nearly everybody's eyes swelled and watered.

We didn't pass notes to other cells because of a self-imposed quarantine. But it made no difference. Guards carried the contaminated pots and pans from one room to the next. After our room had been exposed, we squinted through cracks, saw no guard (or much of anything), and tapped to the next room: "You got it yet?"

"Not yet. . . . Wait a minute. . . . Yeah, we got it."

For two weeks the pink eye rendered us helpless. Some eyes swelled completely shut. Earlier a V medic had entered a contaminated room and had ordered eyedrops put into the prisoners' eyes. Then he came into our cell and shouted, "OK, you criminals, line up."

We had been very careful to avoid the disease and were suspicious of the medication. Five of the guys refused to line up, saying, "No, sir. Not in my eyes. Go away with that stuff."

"Every criminal take medicine!"

They knew the officers weren't going to press it so the five remained adamant. Within the hour, nearly all of us contacted pink eye. The only ones who didn't were the men who had refused.

Diarrhea and dysentery were common. We also had epidemics of infectious hepatitis, but as far as I know, no one died from it. With limited medical background, we also diagnosed what we thought was scurvy, beriberi, malaria, mononucleosis, and pneumonia. Generally, a POW who was close to death was taken out of the room and hospitalized. In many instances, he returned with better health. Some men never returned.

* * *

Except for a puppy or two, we had no pets. We did, however, spend hours lying on our bunks and observing undomesticated animals and insects. Soon we knew the life cycle of the lizard—"zotting" flies or mosquitoes, mating, using strategy while in battle. We tried to tame the lizards and even had names for them, but they were too unpredictable.

Toads surprised us. Common wartridden toads, the kind we had seen in American gardens, were able to waggle up the inside corner of a wall until they reached the ceiling.

There was no way we could avoid ants—all colors, all sizes, biters and nonbiters. One POW said that he once saw a red ant on his sandal—the biggest red ant he'd ever seen, about one-half inch long. He reached down with a stick to brush the ant away. The ant put its front legs on the stick, and as the fellow raised it, the ant picked up the sandal! The prisoner swore that this was truth. Like so many incidents, he could not reenact this ant's show of strength, but he added that to a long list entitled "POW Believe It or Not."

We did, however, observe amazing things about ants. When we saw a trail of ants rushing to some unknown destination, we placed a piece of toilet paper or a leaf across the trail and, after the ants became accustomed, we turned the paper 180 degrees. The ants approached the bridge and, suddenly confronted with a one-way street, they turned around. They refused to cross over, and we speculated that ants must leave some kind of indicator of the direction of travel.

Ants were always bothersome, especially when I tried to save food Wanting to rid myself of these pests, I found a method that was partially successful. I discovered that if I killed a leading ant, the trailing ants immediately turned back without making contact with their victimized leader. After they crawled a foot or so, I squashed the new leader, and again the remaining ants reversed. Rather than going around the first dead ant, they circled randomly between the two.

Thus, I learned that ants avoided dead ants, or perhaps the smell of death. With this knowledge, I smeared ants on my finger and drew a line around my cup. Sure enough, the ants refused to cross the line. My cup was at last free of ants . . . that is, free for about an hour. Apparently, the danger signal wore off, and ants once again besieged my cup.

Oftentimes, my hoarded bread became infested with ants.

I discovered that if I tore the bread into bite-sized pieces, the ants disappeared and I enjoyed their leftovers. There were so many opportunities to gain new knowledge at the University of Hanoi!

The rats were cat-sized monsters—so fat that some could hardly run, and so tough-skinned that they were almost impossible to kill. We threw things at them that would knock a man down, but they returned to their legs and continued wobbling. These curious rats explored everything. Once I awoke to feel a rat nibbling at my nose! Of course I was startled, but fortunately so was the rat.

Rats seldom became aggressive, although some of the fellows had trouble with cornered rats fighting back. When we covered ourselves with mosquito nets at night, we were generally safe from intruders. However, rats occasionally

squeezed inside our nets, and with no easy means of escape, they turned hostile. A prisoner entrapped with the rat had to stand quickly so that the bottom of his net lifted off the bed and permitted the rat's escape.

We devised all kinds of traps. One was a potty turned upside down and held up with a bamboo trigger tied to a string. We placed bread under the potty and waited for the rat to crawl inside. After we trapped the rat the problem was how to get it out. No one wanted to reach in because the rat might be rabid.

Sometimes this dilemma could have come right out of the comics. Picture this: two guys with brooms waiting for the rat to come out; when it does, they hit each other on the head—great white hunters with a watchful gallery. On occasions when the rat was killed, the "big game hunters" posed melodramatically with one foot on rat and high-powered broom over shoulder. If the rat escaped, the gallery cheered. None of us really wanted a dead rat because we had no place to put the carcass except in the *bo*. As soon as the body cooled the lice would desert their host to infest the bucket for days.

During daylight we weren't allowed to use our nets and mosquitoes became a serious problem. We fought them off with hands, and the natural outcome was a mosquito-killing contest. Our rules were that we couldn't slap a mosquito against the wall; instead we had to catch it one-handed while it was in flight. The contest lasted from six to nine in the evenings. At the close of the contest, the three of us in my cell thought we had done pretty well—175 mosquitoes in three hours. We lost. The guys next door caught 206.

inventions

Adaptation to a completely foreign environment was for us a twenty-four-hour-a-day job. We couldn't leave the 4:00 o'clock traffic jam and forget it all. In fact, we were being detained so long that we decided our domain should adapt to us.

When I was first imprisoned, it occurred to me that I could certainly use a radio. From a military viewpoint, of course, a radio would be invaluable, but it would also be a source of entertainment and a tremendous uplift of spirit. How I wished I could pick up the "Voice of America" or BBC or some Philippine broadcast!

I had received a degree in engineering from Annapolis, so I knew something about electronics. I had also been a ham radio operator as a teen-ager. What spurred me on to the idea that I could make a radio, however, was a "bargain" I'd sent for when I was ten years old. For fifteen cents I acquired blueprints for a do-it-yourself radio. The components I would look for in the prison courtyard would be similar to those I'd gathered twenty years earlier.

Each time I went outside, I scanned what was a junk-collector's fertile yard and "lifted" parts. The aerial was easy—a wire strung up high in the room. The ground wire also was no problem—another wire running down to a puddle of water. Finding the other components would take time . . . and luck.

For the detector I found a piece of graphite (pencil lead) and carefully balanced it on two razor blades. The antenna coil was a homemade wooden spool around which I wrapped pieces of electrical wire.

I constructed the capacitor from alternating pieces of tinfoil and waxed paper. The most important, and most difficult, component was the ear piece. For this, I needed an electromagnet, a diaphragm, and the housing.

My electromagnet would be a nail. The housing for the diaphragm would be a little white porcelain insulator that the French had installed decades earlier. To get this piece, all I did was to jiggle the insulator for about ten hours until it worked loose from the wall. I would wrap fine wire around the nail and place it through the center hole of the insulator. Another razor blade would become the diaphragm.

I would pack the whole thing with soap so that the components were tight. I'd spent much time and taken many chances, but it was worth it. The radio was near completion.

And then, guards, during one of their frequent inspections, raided me. The only radio program I would ever hear would be Hanoi Hannah. I still believe it would have worked.

Boredom had free reign in our prison and visited us like a bill collector. We tried to avoid its presence by inventing games. At first, I played solitaire with my postage-stamp playing cards. Several months later other POWs and I laminated layers of cross-grained toilet paper with rice glue. Six or eight of these layers made a very tough cardboard and an excellent acey-ducey board for backgammon. We needed checkers, and so we pinched out the soft center of a bread loaf, poured water on it, kneaded it to form nickle-sized wafers. We colored one team's checkers with red brick dust. Ashes were rubbed into the others to make black.

Backgammon required dice, and the easiest way to make them was to form bread dough into cubes. After a day or so, we punched the correct number of holes in the dice. The little cubes were then concealed and dried for several days. After the drying period, we covered the dough with paint scraped from the wall. For the spots we used tincture of violet.

One problem with these dice was that they would get hot and crack. Several techniques were therefore developed to cure them. Some fellows laid a wet rag over them and even got up in the middle of the night to keep the rag moist. A simpler solution was to add salt to the dough because the dice stayed moist for longer periods of time. Still another solution was to avoid bread dough altogether by grinding down wood, bricks, or pieces of concrete. Once they were completed, we were very careful to roll our dice on cloth or blankets to prevent chipped corners.

We also played chess. The pieces were generally made by chewing chunks of toilet paper into paper-mache and forming them into the desired shape. Ashes and brick dust were again used for coloring, or the pieces were left a natural brown.

* * *

Because of the physical fitness programs and low-calorie soups, many of the POWs had grown thin and were interested in the suit sizes they'd need when they got home. Others wanted to know how much their spines had compressed from the G-force at ejection. (Pilots would sometimes lose an inch in height from the impact.)

As a result of these varied interests we developed our own Bureau of Standards, and several particularly interested prisoners took charge. On one of their bunks was calibrated the "official golden yardstick," an average of known heights or handspans by inches. Letters written on 8½- by 11-inch paper were also used to verify or update our nail scratches. One prisoner stole a straightedge and converted its marked centimeters.

The yardstick established, POWs measured waists and laid separate strings on the rack to see how one more day had built them up or torn them down. A good physique was about the only thing we had to take pride in, and the quarter-inch scratches on the bed board gave meaningful testimony.

All of us had lost weight (some for the better), but we didn't know how much. It took us awhile to figure it out, but we finally devised scales. If we had a large enough water tub, we floated a prisoner and measured the volume of water he displaced. Some of the engineers remembered that water weighed 62.5 pounds per cubic foot, but we were stymied until we received an eight-ounce bottle of shampoo from home and could determine volume. We squeezed the shampoo into drinking cups, measured these containers, and finally determined cubic-foot volume.

This weight scale was too vulnerable, of course, and frequently we had no tank, nor were we allowed enough time for careful measure. Consequently, we made another scale by laying a bed board on a fulcrum, placing a bucket of measured water on one end of the board and a POW on the other. We moved the bucket until the board was balanced,

measured distance to the fulcrum, and applied the moment arms formula.

Another of our continual interests was temperature. We knew if we were hot or cold, but we had no way of determining degrees. I stumbled on to a "thermometer" by accident. Our light source was a naked bulb hanging from approximately six feet of twisted two-conductor cord. I noticed that as the temperature raised the wire expanded and untwisted the cord, causing the bulb to revolve slightly. As the temperature lowered, the wire contracted. It was only necessary for us to put a mark on the bulb and to graduate the hairline shadow it cast on the floor. We could tell when the temperature was near zero by seeing ice crystals forming on bath water, but we never had a feel for summer heat.

Nor could we tell the time of day. The banging of the morning gong depended on how late the Vietnamese caroused the night before. Since most of our cups leaked, a water clock was easy to devise. Our problem with this was that as the water level decreased, the drops decelerated, making the instrument even less accurate. We tried burning punk to keep track of time, but that didn't work too well either because of the various sizes and qualities of paper and the changing humidity.

I decided the best timer was an actual clock, and so I started collecting the necessary parts for an improvised grandfather clock: four-inch pieces of wire, spaghetti insulation taken off electrical wire, bamboo sticks, a bob weight. The escape mechanism was the most difficult, but after weeks of experimentation, I completed a clock which worked with fair precision for a maximum of sixty minutes. This was more than enough time to satisfy the necessary requirement—the five minutes allowed the speakers in our Toastmasters Club.

The relentlessly cold winters forced us to initiate some weird projects to keep warm. I wanted a thick, form-fitting hat, so I saved all the rags I could find. I tore these into quarter-inch strips, tied them together, and wound them into grapefruit-sized balls. With bamboo needles, I started knitting around and around until I had a circle the size of a big pancake. I then put it over my head and measured for ear flaps. Fifteen balls of yarn and a few dropped stitches later I completed my hat. I was proud of my creation because, even though it didn't look like much from a distance, close up it showed a neat herringbone pattern.

The Vietnamese didn't approve. They disregarded my pleas, took it, and threw it in the junk pile outside. The next time I got out, however, I sneaked over and recovered it. That hat was a savior, keeping my ears from aching.

On important occasions we made wine. Except for citrus, any fruit or vegetable was used—rice, banana, pear, apple. Often the fruits were already rotten by the time we got them, but it didn't matter. We scoured our potties, tossed in the fruit, added water (and sugar if we had it), and waited about fourteen days for the bubbles to stop. For each success we had many failures—from straight vinegar to sewage which stunk to high heaven. We could actually discern the alcohol, and some of the guys drank the stuff no matter what. I'm surprised we didn't come home with jake leg.

insanity

The first I knew of it was in the fall of 1968, and I didn't understand. An old beat-up French ambulance rattled into the courtyard, and an American wearing prison garb crawled out. He weaved like a robot, with head down and shoulders slumped. It was odd. Guards never allowed POWs to walk that way. We doubled-timed.

Who was this man? Had he just come from the hospital? Was he tortured into semiconsciousness, or was he faking? When would we find out?

Our comm net was poor, and for a full month my cellmates and I pondered the meaning of this incident. The month ended, and from Stable to Pigsty No. 1 came a message from the SRO: "Attention, everyone. Who can give information about mental instability? We have a problem and request help soon." Over 150 prisoners in the Zoo held bachelor's and master's degrees, and the officer had hoped that someone in the group would have a background in psychiatry.

Locked in Pigsty, we separately considered the question and jointly concluded that our discussions were of no use until we had more specific details about the symptoms. "What's the problem?" read our response to the Stable.

Three days later we received an answer:

"POW here with extreme withdrawal. Won't eat or talk. Belligerent. Please offer suggestions."

It was a serious undertaking to recommend treatment for an unknown illness. Did his eyes dilate? What did he do with his hands? What did the officer mean by "belligerent"?

After several weeks and a few more notes, it became apparent that the man's condition was worsening. We could, on rare occasions, see him being taken to bathe. Each trip showed him more haggard.

Messages from the Stable became urgent. The man was hallucinatory, insisting that his cellmates were Communists pieced together with the limbs and heads of dead Americans. "Whose arm is that?" he asked. "Is that my pilot's arm?" "How can you Commies speak such good English?"

Because this sick man was wasting away, it was necessary for his cellmates to force-feed him. The hostile patient was still strong, requiring four or five men to constrain him so that a bamboo stick could be forced between his teeth. Another prisoner mashed rice down his throat. When they finished, he would gag himself to regurgitate what he thought was poison from the Communists, spewing rice all over the room.

He was entranced. When a V entered the room, he refused to bow. Angered, a guard screamed, "Bow! Bow!" and whipped his fist across the expressionless face. The man continued to stand. The guards continued to beat him unmercifully.

His cellmates knew that such brutality exacerbated his

condition. So when the guard entered, a cellmate would stand on either side of the man, another at his back, and a fourth close enough to punch him hard in the abdomen. At the signal the four men would physically force him to bow. The Vietnamese accepted this conduct.

As a consequence, the man became more hostile toward his cellmate "Communists." He spit in their faces, hit them with his fists, and kicked. No longer was it safe for all the men to sleep at the same time.

A "Rat Patrol" was established. The men took shifts of two hours (or as near two hours as they could determine). The vigil lasted throughout each night, with one man pacing

back and forth, back and forth, guarding his seven sleeping comrades and himself from the demented POW.

Tension increased. Life in a Hanoi prison cell was already too grueling for the prisoners to have to endure more stress. Any vestige of composure in the cellmates showed signs of erosion. Some of them—particularly those who were still recovering from cuts and bruises (the reward for their sacrifices)—argued, "Why should we die because of him? He's no longer a human being. Do you want to be his first victim?"

The senior officer, still in good control, answered, "No, we're going to help him. He is our comrade. He is on our side even if he doesn't know it. We have to force him to bow. We have to make him eat. We have to wash him. We have to keep him alive."

The senior officer pleaded with the V to do something: "For God's sake, send the man home! Find someone who can befriend him! Give him medical treatment!"

Eventually the V officer acknowledged the severity of the situation by saying, "We machine at hospital put charge electricity through brain. Due to lenient, humane treatment by Vietnamese people, cure criminal."

They took him away, and the cell was quiet for a month. Messages continued back and forth. One morning we heard a vehicle enter camp—it was the ambulance. The man stepped out. This time we saw more bounce to his step. He never smiled, but he wasn't a robot. All of us were grateful.

The guards led him back to his old cell where his cellmates—unsure of the right approach—wanted him to know he was a part of them: "It's nice to have you back! We're going to have a good time today! We'll play some games and tell stories to one another!"

The man smiled.

The afternoon meal came, and included on the menu was a special treat—one banana for each POW. The men remembered how much their friend loved bananas, and as a kind gesture each gave his banana to the returned comrade.

He had nine bananas, and he ate every one of them. Shortly after, he got sick. Suddenly he shouted, "You are poisoning me, you Communists!" and he stuck his finger down his throat to regurgitate the "poison."

The comrade regressed to the same state as before—withdrawal, refusal to eat, hostility toward cellmates. The Vietnamese brought in a plastic cloth to cover his body when he was fed. They gave him rice with chunks of meat, and his cellmates continued to force food down his throat.

The senior officer pleaded once more to the V to send the man home or, since he had returned with slight improvement, to take him back to the hospital. A month later, and an exhausting nine months from his first day at the Stable, the man was again taken to the hospital.

Every six months or so, we saw our sick POW comrade transported between solitary confinement and the hospital. We felt helpless; the only way we could assist was with prayer. After September 1970, we never saw him again.

charade

Palmer got his idea from watching our mentally sick comrade. He needed that idea, because he had crawled to the end of his branch and couldn't bring himself to come back down.

It was the spring of 1969. Palmer, Bob, and I knew every identifiable trait in our cells and in ourselves. Except for the unfolding tragedy of our friend who suffered mental anguish a courtyard distant, we had little to talk about. Not that talking would have helped much. Palmer, staunchly patriotic to the American cause, preferred silence to Bob's more radical viewpoints.

Palmer was a tough hombre. He grew up in the rough sections of San Diego and Burbank and still bore street-fight scars. His mother frequently changed husbands, and her son was shuttled so often that identification with his surroundings was impractical. As a result, Palmer was a maverick who took pride in self-determination. He rebelled against anything that resembled authority, and even at one point had "hogged" with the Hell's Angels. He was strong, spending four or five hours a day keeping his body in shape with push-ups and sit-ups. He was also strong-willed, or at least that was the impression he wanted to give.

Nevertheless, harsh imprisonment required life-sustaining dependence on the Vietnamese. Palmer had undergone the same treatment that we all had experienced during our first few weeks. He too had given the V more than name, rank, serial number, and date of birth. Interrogators had asked about his childhood and he had responded with lies.

A year after I was shot down, the V camp commander decided that POWs should complete an autobiography and acquired special forms for that purpose. Officers then escorted each of us to the quiz-room to answer a question-naire we called the *Bluebook*.

Our senior officer, Major Larry Guarino, had decided earlier that there was no point in being tortured for telling the price of our tennis rackets (one of the questions). He notified us to fill out the questionnaire if we wanted, and told us not to worry about giving information useless to the V in their war effort. V officers never seemed to check our answers anyway, and when it was my turn, I didn't hesitate to answer: tennis racket—$2.50; yearly income—$1500.00.

Palmer, however, wasn't happy about the camp com-mander's order because he couldn't remember all the lies he'd told the year before. So he decided not to fill out the book. Needing to reassure us and himself of his individuality, he flaunted this refusal in front of the guards. That was a big mistake. The guards reacted by making him stand on his knees for two days with his hands up in the air—a common self-torture technique.

After the torture the officers approached Palmer, but

again he refused to write. Instead, he fell off his stool and rolled into a tight ball and didn't seem at all bothered by the subsequent beatings. Palmer was indeed a tough hombre.

The beatings became more severe, and Palmer knew he couldn't withstand torture indefinitely. He'd backed himself into a corner, and yet he was not going to acquiesce. To him the only recourse left was to continue the protest under pretense: feigned insanity. He practiced the walk and actions of the man from the Stable. He listened carefully as neighboring prisoners tapped out the symptoms of psychosis. There would be no mistake: V officers would be made to correlate his faked demeanor with the behavior of the sick man. He stopped bathing and cleaning around his bunk. He pretended to quit eating, leaving his own soup bowl untouched while he ate from ours. He became a catatonic zombie, spending the day entranced on his rack. He waited for and wanted guards to notice. When they came, he stared with glassy eyes and breathed heavily with open mouth. His thick black beard added to the enigma.

Instead of bowing when guards entered, Palmer pretended he didn't see them. As they beat him for refusing to bow, he crawled under his bunk and rolled into a ball. But he was an inveterate optimist. If only he could hold out for just two more weeks, he'd be going home and would escape his dilemma. Or so he thought.

Two weeks passed, and there was no sign of repatriation. Palmer couldn't bear the terrible thought of extended imprisonment. Guards weren't buying his playact as he had planned; instead they increased surveillance of our cell. His once active body yearned for exercise, but his self-imposed shackles wouldn't let him. His restrictions were about to drive him into actual insanity, and for a solution, he asked

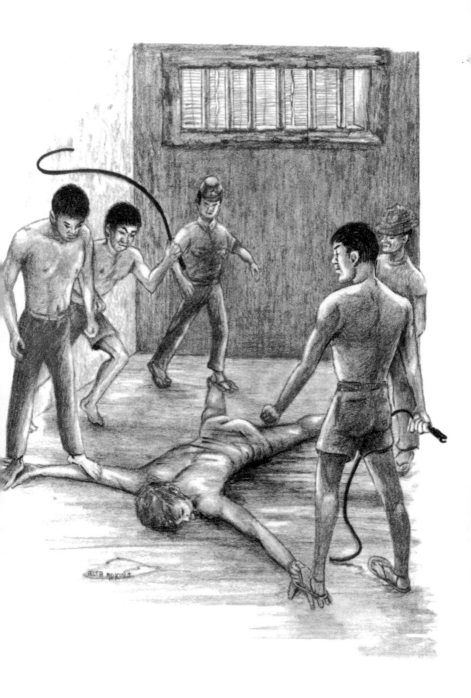

Bob and me to watch the door so that he could sneak a cup of water or rush through a few push-ups.

I was senior officer in the cell and told Palmer that if he had to play crazy, he should be more subtle about it. Bob and I were getting tired of doing his work—having to maintain constant guard at the door and sharing an already meager portion of food. But Palmer wouldn't listen. All it took was the rattle of a truck or the jingle of keys and he thought we were going home.

Tension increased. Palmer alienated himself further by refusing to speak to us. His unwashed body reeked. We began to wonder if his charade was real.

Bob and I informed Korean ace Jim Kasler, the SRO in the next cell, of the latest developments. V officers, still not knowing how to interpret Palmer's shenanigans, started taking me to the quiz room and asking whether Palmer was really crazy. I told the camp commander that I didn't know, that Palmer wasn't talking to me either.

When I returned to my cell, Bob gave me the news: "We'd better batten down the hatches, Plumber. I was tapping to Jim and didn't see a guard peek in. Palmer did, though, and when the guard ran around to Jim's cell, Palmer sat up to warn us and pounded the danger signal on the wall. What he didn't know was that another guard saw him do it. Now what're we gonna do?" I looked over and saw that Palmer had reassumed his crazy act. All we could do was wait.

As soon as the guards could inform them, the V officers went to Jim's cell and led him to the quiz room. They figured that Jim had ordered Palmer to feign insanity and tortured the ace with rubber-tire whips in an attempt to get a confession. At the same time, officers came into our cell, ordered the guards to slap Bob and me around, and then made the two of us stand on our knees with our hands held high.

Several hours passed. We were in a ticklish situation. Being ordered to stay on designated spots with hands up, we were taking chances when we got up to clear the door. It was impossible to be hustling back to our spots on knees and still appear innocent.

The V couldn't break Jim to confess. The unsuccessful officers then had to save face and suggested to Jim that Palmer be given another chance to fill out the bluebook. Jim agreed, knowing Palmer wouldn't do it.

We heard the four or five guards and two officers return Jim to his cell. His cell door remained open and we knew the V were inside. Then on our wall we heard "shave and a haircut," our coded call-up signal: tap . . . tap, tap, tap . . . tap.

We knew Jim had been forced to communicate and we didn't answer. Again, tap . . . tap, tap, tap . . . tap, louder this time. We stayed at our spots.

Soon, an officer came to our cell and shouted, "Answer call!" We bowed and, pretending to be puzzled, responded, "What call?"

"On wall. Kasler calling you."

"Who's Kasler?"

"Answer the call!"

"Sorry. We don't hear anything."

The officer walked back to Jim's room, and the next thing we heard was a really loud "shave and a haircut." Two officers returned to our door, opened the flap, and again ordered, "Answer call from Kasler! Important message for you."

"We don't know the signal."

The officers called a guard. We heard the jangling of keys,

a sound which struck terror in the heart of every POW. The officers entered and demanded, "Answer call!"

"We don't hear call."

A guard ran back to Jim's cell and pounded the call-up. The officers, furious by this time, screamed, "Answer that call!"

I responded, "I don't know the code. How do you answer?"

"You know! You answer!"

By this time the guards were getting nasty, throwing fists to our faces. Finally Bob went to the wall and pounded twice. The officers crowded around, and Jim tapped the camp commander's order. The officers said, "OK. You got message. Tell it crazy man." With that, they walked out. They had "saved face."

The jig was up for Palmer. The V were convinced that he had been acting. They needed no more proof than his pounding on the wall.

The next morning guards entered the cell and started beating Palmer on the head. Immediately he rolled under his bunk and into a ball. They poked and jabbed, but they couldn't get him to come out.

Another day passed; and the guards, seeing that they were at an impasse, changed their tactics: "Come out! Today you take bath."

Palmer crawled from under his bunk and Bob and I led him out the door. At the bath area we stripped naked and then we went through the same motions that had been performed at the Stable. We undressed Palmer, led him to the water, and started scrubbing down his body.

At that moment, it seemed as though the entire V army stepped out from every door in the courtyard carrying sticks, hoes, rifles, hand grenades. The officer ordered Bob and me to get dressed and to return immediately to our cells. We didn't want to leave Palmer, but we had no choice.

Now he was really on his own. He didn't have his bunk to crawl under. Guards from every side grabbed him, threw him to the ground, and started beating him unmercifully with clubs. They tied his wrists and feet and hauled him away hanging from a bamboo pole like a jungle boar.

Bob and I were back in our cell, and for several hours we didn't know what was happening. Then from Kasler's room came a message which had originated from the other end of camp: "Palmer in solo. Six by six room. Four feet high. Solid walls. No vent. Torture continues."

* * *

A month later, Palmer returned. Dejected, he told us how he had been tortured until he aided V propaganda by preparing tapes about good treatment. He had also written letters to this effect to Senator Fulbright and President Nixon. He had made a mistake. He had been brutally tortured and had caused other prisoners pain. He was sorry for what he'd done, and he apologized.

Palmer was no longer a tough hombre.

escape

It happened during the Palmer charade. My third cell-mate, Bob Wideman, had been taken out to be interrogated and was in leg irons in a cell near the gate. Just the two of us—Palmer and I—remained. That was important.

We had often discussed the possibility of escape but had put it in the backs of our minds because Bob had promised that if we did escape, he would sit tight on his bunk without moving. Even if we were successful, he alone would be left to face the irate V.

It was Saturday night, 10 May 1969, and it was raining. Most of the guards had gone to town, leaving a skeleton crew. This unmotivated gaggle, none too vigilant when sober, often drank or smoked their troubles into oblivion. And none of them liked to get wet.

We had some civilian clothes. We had jimmied the bars in the vent—loose enough to break and yet tight enough to appear unmolested. Palmer and I felt the tingle. The thought of freedom permeated our reflexes with a warm electricity. Palmer was still pretending to be insane, but the storm had knocked the lights out and we could whisper without fear of retribution.

"Hey, Charlie, tonight's the night. We've got the clothes, and we can disguise ourselves as some kind of foreign visitors."

"Yeah, but how do we get out of town?"

"We'll lay low during the day and move at night. We've got that bread yet, and I've saved some rice."

I remembered the order from Captain Stockdale two years previous: "No escape without outside help." Our senior officers had never rescinded that order. I ached with doubts, and Palmer pressed for consent. Still, discretion set up too many obstacles. We couldn't let emotion outrun reason. I paused.

"I don't know, Palmer; chances are we'd never make it out of the city. We'd better not." It was a long time before I fell asleep.

Early the next morning, a shave and a haircut was our alarm. It was the comm call-up:

"Last night two bolted from Annex! No details." We were astounded. The Annex was adjacent to the Zoo, separated only by a ten-foot wall.

We fired a message back: "Request more info." We knew that if they had made it over the perimeter wall, they must have had several hours to squeeze along city alleyways. Had I been wrong? Had Palmer and I missed the chance? Was last night the night?

Then it hit the fan. The V started at the Annex and proceeded to inspect thoroughly every cell and storeroom in the camp. When they entered our cell, we knew they meant business. They took our civilian clothes, all remnants of

packages, candy, gum, razor blades. They tore apart the shutters to find my stolen book of essays. They discovered Pigsty's faulty vent bars, but they did not attribute the loosened condition to us. I was thankful that we had taken the precautions.

Frequent messages unfolded the story. We learned that the escape was no spur-of-the-moment plan. These two prisoners had prepared for over a year, during which time they gathered comm devices, all kinds of camouflage, food, plastic water containers, and shivs made of filed metal. They took along iodine for water purification. They had searched the area and prepared maps. They had stolen two V conical hats, two chogy poles, shovels. The only thing they needed was a dark, rainy Saturday night. Then it came.

The cell in the Annex had a small hole in its sixteen-foot ceiling which the French had built as an access to the attic. By standing on the shoulders of two cellmates on bedboards, the men had reached into the hole to store their contraband. The lighting system was old and the wiring so poor that lights were always going out, particularly during thundershowers.

Shortly after midnight the two men broke the bulb to insure darkness. They were then lifted into the attic where they painted their faces with iodine and ashes, changed into V clothing, and pulled conical hats over Caucasian eyes. At one o'clock they were ready.

They prayed that the guard, standing watch somewhere in the courtyard below, was half asleep or high on dope.

Slowly, carefully, they removed rectangles of flat, clay tile and placed them on the wet roof beside the jagged opening. Suddenly, a tile was jarred from its resting position and began to gain momentum as it clattered down the slippery rooftop. A frantic grasp for the clay judas was too late! The tile struck the concrete below and shattered.

The men froze. Was it too late to remove their camouflage and return to their cell? No, the iodine was too permanent. The attempt would be as incriminating as the deed. They waited.

For fifteen minutes they waited . . . and heard nothing. They removed another tile and climbed cautiously onto the roof. Crouched, they slipped to the roof's edge and down a lightning rod. Cellmates, glued to cracks, could see the men scuttle to a lean-to, climb it, and disappear over the perimeter wall. They made it! Now short in number, the remaining men crawled under their nets and prayed hard for a successful escape and for their own ability to endure. Every sound jolted their nerves. There was no sleep.

At five o'clock Sunday morning Magoo was up to make his rounds. He calmly opened the cell door and yelled "Uh! Uh!" to rouse POWs from beneath their nets. The cellmates climbed out slowly, shuffled to their assigned spots and bowed. Magoo counted, "Mot, hai, ba, bon, nam, sau, bay . . . tam? . . ." There were supposed to be *chin*. Magoo lifted the nets. Prisoners stood tight-jawed, their prayers unworded. "Bay . . . bay," and all bunks were empty!

Magoo ran out and locked the cell.

The news raced from wall to wall. In a matter of minutes, the latest developments were relayed through fifteen cells to Pigsty I. Before all the questions could be answered, however, the day was spent. We usually didn't communicate on Sundays, but this was certainly cause for exception. Our spirits lifted to know that someone would soon be able to tell the ugly story of V brutality.

On Monday, 12 May, Bob moved back into our cell. Palmer and I were puzzled. We had assumed he would be gone for a long time—the V had put him in irons to try to force his admission of Palmer's sanity.

As soon as the guards left, Bob told us, "Boy, did I see a strange thing early yesterday morning. The guards were running around in the courtyard like crazy at about five o'clock, and pretty soon all kinds of high-rankers showed up. Then this jeep pulled up and two guys got out. I couldn't tell who they were. I'm not sure if they were Americans or V; in fact, they looked so beat up and ragged I could barely tell that they were human beings. And the funny thing about it was that the V started taking all kinds of junk out of the jeep and laying it on the ground. There was tinfoil and rags and pieces of mirrors and plastic bags. I can't understand it!"

"What happened to the guys who got out of the jeep?" I asked.

"I don't know for sure. The V took them into a cell, and I didn't see them again."

That afternoon via the comm net we were told that the two men who had escaped had been captured and brought back in a jeep. They were taken to a cell, tortured, and again put into the jeep and hauled away. The last comm message was from Major Guarino, our commander: "All hands join in prayer for our two men in trouble."

About that time, all hell broke loose in the Annex. First, the officers escorted each of the seven remaining prisoners to the torture room. I winced when I heard that the V were employing the "fanbelt." I had endured this twice, being lashed fifteen or twenty times. Some of these men, however, were subjected to seven or eight hundred lashings over a period of two weeks. I wondered how any human being undergoing such horror could live.

The V officers then took the senior men out of each Annex cell and stripped them to lie spread-eagle on the dirt floor in preparation for still more "strong arm." Next on the list were the comm teams.

Each prisoner involved with Annex comm was beaten until he told the name of the receiver in the adjacent cell. There was no point in lying: the wrong man would be tortured. Most of us in the network had volunteered for that role and were aware of the consequences.

The next several weeks we kept getting reports. "So-and-so is being tortured now." Palmer, Bob, and I could only wait, knowing that our time was coming. We were glad that we were so far removed from the Annex.

During this period of wholesale torture, the V decided that, since they had all the machinery out, they might as well crack the Palmer case. They called me out. Probably the most horrible experience in my life was having to sit on the grill in the quiz room and hear Americans in the next room cry for mercy. The interrogators asked, "You know sound? You know who next? You!"

One day we were alerted to a message over the comm net which stated that our own classified information had been compromised and several lies had been told. The V had figured that the escape was a wide-scale plot, involving all the POWs in the camp. They had been mutilating prisoners to make them confess which room would be next. Someone had to answer their question, "Where ready escape room?"

Comforting in the remoteness of Pigsty, we were informed of the contrived answer: "The cell farthest from Annex is the next escape room. Pigsty I!" Our hearts jumped to our throats.

Two weeks prior to this confession, the V had taken our civilian clothing, had confiscated my book, and had discovered the loosened bars. But they were still in such a frenzy and their organization was so poor that they didn't put two and two together. Somewhere along the line they had lost the records of what they had found in Pigsty I.

Otherwise, our cell would have become Trouble City. An angel must have been sitting on our shoulders. The V saw nothing awry and didn't pursue the lie to completion. Palmer and I were glad we hadn't bolted after all.

Altogether, twenty-five men at the Zoo were flayed until their backs and buttocks were a solid mass of blood. One prisoner's finger was severed. Ten were put in irons for six months (the right leg of one man shackled to the left leg of the next). Some had had no prior knowledge of the escape.

Of course, we prayed daily for the two men who were still missing. We assumed that they had been taken to the Hilton and the most sophisticated torture equipment. Several months later, one of the two men returned—hallucinatory and close to death, the result of twenty-seven consecutive days of hell. As far as we knew, the second man had been given the same treatment, but he never came back.

It took several months for the escapee to convalesce. After his physical and mental health returned, he had much apologizing to do. He had done his best. He had done the thing he thought was right. But he didn't make it out of the city.

The two men had traveled until daylight and had crouched in water behind some brush. An old Vietnamese woman, going to the little stream to fill her bucket, spotted the men in weird attire and immediately pointed them out to her comrades. The trip back to the Zoo was no more than five miles.

After that we didn't think much about escape—not that it would be impossible but that the aftermath for the remaining prisoners would be too horrible. We would wait until all of us were safely home before we told our story.

faith

"Thy will be done."

It seemed presumptuous to try to change God's will—to make a "deal" with the Omnipotent. If I promised to devote my life to the ministry in exchange for freedom and failed to follow through—what then? No, trying to bargain with God was unfitting.

From the beginning I offered prayers of acceptance. I remembered the experience of seeing the Christlike shadow in the Green Knobby Room and the comfort I felt in that time of great need. That day I asked God for strength to endure whatever hardship I might face, and I prayed for Anne—not for her fidelity or success but for tolerance, courage, and most of all her happiness . . . with or without me. I continued to pray this prayer daily.

Already I had been blessed. After solitary confinement early in my imprisonment, I was fortunate to have as a cellmate a good Christian man, Kay Russell. We talked a lot

about God and his purpose for us. In family tradition, Kay and I said our prayers together.

One of the first pieces of communication I had received in solitary was from Bob Shumaker. With tugs on the wire, he announced, "Church call is five coughs." I tugged back, "Do we all go to church together?"

"Yes."

I waited excitedly for Sunday morning, thinking that we could gather in the same courtyard to read the Bible and sing hymns. I sang a few hymns to myself to get my voice in shape.

Sunday came, and outside my vent I heard five forced coughs. It suddenly dawned on me that this church call meant that each of us was to begin his worship alone. In our individual cells we united in prayer. Even though we couldn't see or hear one another, we were "two or three gathered together" and He was with us.

In subsequent cells, I joined others in discussions concerning the Bible, religious philosophies, and meaningful sermons. Some of the men were sensitive about their beliefs, so we were careful to avoid theological arguments.

In November 1970 we were happy to be able to discuss, joke, and laugh together in our larger cells, but it was especially rewarding to join for prayer in person. The senior officer began to make assignments: communications, food, health, custodial care, etc. Several of the men in the fifty-seven-man cell were old friends of mine, and when it was time for nominations for chaplain, they submitted my name. The senior officer approached me and asked if I would accept the position. I told him that I would be honored to do so, but that I wasn't a walking Bible and would need assistance.

Several other men were experienced Christians, and

various areas of responsibility evolved somewhat naturally. Kay Russell was choir director, and Tom Barrett was in charge of special Catholic services. My assignment was to coordinate the services and to lead or appoint men for the Sunday worship.

During these covert services we prayed two prayers, the first a general prayer for our comrades, for the sick and injured, for the soldiers in South Viet Nam, and for the North Vietnamese. The second was a special prayer, stemming from my training at the Naval Academy. The chaplain there always included a prayer for the Navy, and from this practice I designed a prayer especially for loved ones awaiting our return.

From the first POW who stepped onto North Vietnamese soil on 5 August 1964, prisoners had been asking for improved treatment . . . better food, clothing, shelter, medical care, books, etc. At the top of the list, however, was always the Bible and permission to hold church services. Over the years the V consented to better food and shelter, but they adamantly rejected our requests for a Bible and Christian fellowship. Since our general life-styles had improved somewhat by 1971, and since our unity provided greater bargaining power, we decided to press the issue.

It had been necessary during our church services to post a man at the door to be sure that no V would see us in prayer. Our service was always very quiet and short, and when a guard did come around we had to break up, whether during prayer or sermonette. The situation was certainly not conducive to meditation.

Thousands of Bibles had been sent to us from church groups all over the world, but the V gave us none. Asking wasn't enough, so we decided to go on a hunger strike. Our senior officer informed the V that we simply didn't want any more food until we could have a Bible and uninterrupted worship. They retaliated by shutting off our drinking water.

To counter this move I devised a small tube from electrical wire insulation and ran it from our vent along the outside wall. After several hours of maneuvering, I finally connected: the tube reached the vent of the room next to ours. The prisoners next door drank half-rations and funneled their remaining water down the tube to trickle into our cups.

The V continually harassed us and pulled out our senior men one by one and put them in solitary confinement. The next ranking officer would always step forward, take command, and continue the fight.

After a few days the V were ready to settle, and so were we. They would give us a church service *if* we abided by certain stipulations. The service would be held according to their schedule. No one could sing, no one could stand, and everyone would adhere strictly to camp regulations. Every word spoken in the "ceremony" was to be written down for the censor's perusal. After all the restrictions, we hadn't gained much; but at least the V had given an inch.

A few weeks later the V saw that our services were not militant and relaxed restrictions. They permitted a four-man choir to sing two hymns. Most important, they gave us a Bible for two days.

Since I was chaplain, I was given charge of this precious book. We set up two-man teams to copy simultaneously adjoining pages. The teams worked furiously, using V pencils and paper and even toilet tissue in a race against the clock. Thirty-six hours later, we had to abandon our work and the book was returned to its dusty shelf.

Of the fifty-seven men in our room, three professed to be atheists and did not participate in the worship. When I talked with them and found how sensitive they were about their philosophy, I decided I was in no position to proselyte. After the V gave us a Bible, a number of prisoners wanted to do nothing more than touch it. I was especially happy to see the three atheists among the first to lay their hands on the opened pages.

Each Christmas the V ordered us to listen to a tape of a V Catholic priest giving a sermon in his native tongue. An interpretor translated it into English, a phrase at a time: "We gather here of the occasion so to celebrate birth of Christ . . . which we do so many years. . . . This time we have special reason . . . multitudes of people are killed and injured . . . by bombs you American pilots drop. . . . You are instrument of devil. . . . Hope is for you and hope for world. . . . Jesus came to save world. . . . Now your opportunity, you American aggressors. . . . You commit sin, but if repent them now, will be clean white like snow. . . . You be able go forward in life. . . . Admit wrongdoing and thank Jesus . . . who born in lowly manger fight oppression from evil aggressors."

It was questionable that the interpretor was deciphering exactly the words of the priest. We knew that translators often lied. In any case it was regretful to hear such a travesty of our Christian belief.

Some Vietnamese officers and guards were very curious about our religion. Occasionally a guard would genuflect and point to us and then to himself to indicate that he was Catholic. These guards seemed more sympathetic in their treatment.

The large majority of V were not Catholic, however, and when they discovered us in prayer (as they did only the last year), they asked, "What you derive from this thing God?" We tried to explain that we received strength, comfort, help, and the promise of eternal life. These concepts were too difficult for them, yet many seemed interested and did not mock our beliefs as "Sacrilege" had done eight years before.

"Sacrilege" was one of the most sadistic guards POWs ever encountered. One of the first men to be shot down was a Catholic. During his capture, the guard stripped him of everything he had, including a rosary. The guard took the rosary, wrapped it around his penis, and blasphemed back and forth in front of the captive. Hence, his name.

To the diehard V Communist, the State was God—their truth, their way, their light. The controlling body in government decreed infallible canons without fear of correction. Whenever peasants asked "Who is the state?" they were told that they themselves were and that they had control in making decisions. Each was told he was a part of the omniscient state. He was, as long as he didn't interfere.

I consider my confinement in prison to be spiritually beneficial. I was given an opportunity that few men have—the time to pause, to reflect, and to establish priorities. I found that my previous value system was unrealistic. Stripped of all my material wealth, the only beacon I could home in on was my faith in an unchanging God.

22

patriotism

We knew that when the V told us something about our country, we could turn those statements 180 degrees and come closer to the truth. They, who idolized our War of Independence, said to us, "In 1776, you have great war revolution, and now we have it, too. President Ho Chi Minh just like George Washington. Just like British put army men in your house, took tax without right, now American warmongers do same thing in South Viet Nam. You neocolonialists crazed by hope of world hegemony."

Instead of destroying our patriotism, the V in fact enhanced our faith in and love for the United States. Their deceptions gave us further reason to unite. (I feel that some of our bombing in North Viet Nam had the same effect on them. In the final analysis, however, our thrust during December 1972 broke their will to continue the war.)

Even if the V had not unintentionally bolstered our morale, our pride in our homeland would have continued. We knew that the U.S. military was the best in the world. We had flown the most sophisticated aircraft from awesome floating hangers. We had learned precision teamwork with the other pilots in our outfits. Although we no longer had these things, we had our memories, and pride in our country remained steadfast.

Of course, we spent much time discussing our homeland, its geography and its history. Some prisoners who had studied political science taught us governmental systems and interpreted developments. Lieutenant Colonel Van Loan was especially helpful when he explained in essays political conduct and its ramifications, especially concerning the war. His positive and logical comments helped us maintain confidence and a spirit of hope.

Although we never became despondent, we did have times of waning morale. One of them was just before the election in 1968. President Johnson stopped the bombing, and we thought that a settlement was near. Instead, nothing happened. Negotiators wasted three months trying to decide the shape of a table, and the V continued painting a picture of a guilty America. That winter was so bleak that we counted only three or four days of sunshine. During this depressing period men like Jack Van Loan and Charlie Southwick, senior officers who had better perspective and more stability, were instrumental in keeping us on the right track.

We memorized the Preamble to the Constitution and the Gettysburg Address. We tried to collect all the Bills of Rights and patriotic quotes. One we found especially meaningful was Patrick Henry's: "Is life so dear, or peace so sweet, as to be purchased at the price of chains and slavery? Forbid it, Almighty God! I know not what course others may take, but as for me, give me liberty, or give me death!"

We were willing to stay until the war had run its course. We were willing to pay the price if true peace could be purchased. But in the winter of 1968 and 1969 we needed to know that something was going on. If the bombing had stopped and the negotiations were getting nowhere, what were we doing in prison?

Some POWs were superpatriots, feeling the United States could do no wrong. A few felt that we had made a mistake and that it was time for us to get out. With most of the prisoners, I accepted the fact that we were not perfect, but felt that we were fighting for a worthy cause and should persevere to the end. We believed in our country's heritage—in the men who had shed blood, sweat, and tears in order to build a great nation. We wanted to be counted in that number.

The war in Viet Nam was more political than military, which accounted for the seeming ineffectiveness of our far superior military strength. If we had applied our tremendous firepower, the war would have been over in a matter of hours. At the same time, however, a nation would have been smoldering ashes. Our policy was clear. Great efforts were made to preserve the lives and property of civilians. Pilots were threatened with court-martial if they failed to pinpoint accurately military targets, even to the extent that they jeopardized their own lives by swooping just above treetops to preserve a peasant hut fifty yards from a SAM radarscope. The V, capitalizing on this, made targets especially difficult by placing their military equipment in the middle of peasant hamlets or next to schools. In fact, several antiaircraft artillery guns were stationed on hospital rooftops.

I feel the U.S. involvement in the war was for several reasons. First, we had a commitment to help underdeveloped nations if they wanted help. Our ally South Viet Nam was about to be victimized by the same Communist strategy that had been occurring since World War II. Unless we did something, it soon would be another Hungary, Cuba, or Albania. The U.S. took a stand in Korea, and that worked for a long time. Our next stand was in Viet Nam.

The war was a show of credibility, of example. The most powerful free nation in history could not idly watch the Communist world gobble up and dissolve sovereign nations. We had to play the surgeon to excise the malignant disease of mind control.

I don't condone war. I think there are few justifiable reasons for killing. In Viet Nam, war was a last-ditch effort of international diplomacy. It was difficult to justify my six years of imprisonment when politicians, with expense-paid trips to Paris, should have solved the problems through negotiation. In this case, our negotiators were at the end of their rope. The Communists didn't understand anything but the big hammer. When our B52s shattered Hanoi's defenses with thousands of bombs, the V realized we meant business.

I believe that historians will record our efforts in Viet Nam as having taken the claws out of Communism. In the 1950s, the Communists were ready to go into any underdeveloped nation in the world to provoke a revolution. They no longer exhibit such an intense interest because they fear they will be dealing with the same nation that had the tenacity to spend ten years defending tiny Viet Nam. I see President Nixon's trips to Peking and Moscow as definite evidence that the Viet Nam war demonstrated this credibility and proved to Communist nations that the only way to maintain harmony is through peaceful coexistence.

I didn't go into the war with a ready-made political philosophy. In fact I was so bent on being a good Naval officer and pilot who knew my equipment that I had little time to ponder the philosophy of it all. My feelings were formulated in prison camps, admittedly with few observations other than the reading between lines of Communist newspapers.

We wanted and needed to love our homeland. We sang "America, the Beautiful" and the national anthem whenever we could. We faced east once a week and pledged our allegiance. We contrasted our Bill of Rights and Constitution to the Communist Manifesto. Daily, we saw how "Big Brother" destroyed individuality.

We compared our lot with that of the guards. While POWs were behind bars, the V were captives inside their own bamboo borders. We considered ourselves more fortunate than they. One day we'd leave *our* cells.

holidays

"You are in Caesar's Palace and are just entering a large banquet hall reserved in your honor. Johnnie, Bob, and all your other friends are present; they hush for a moment and then applaud as you make your way to the head table. You ask them to be seated, and Gina Lollabrigida and Marilyn Monroe take their places at either side. You notice the decor of the room and the table—crystal chandeliers, plush carpeting, embroidered linen tablecloth, white bone china, expensive goblets, and tableware of gold.

"Tuxedoed waiters serve the dinner: caviar and artichoke hearts and kippered herring, pheasant under glass, lobster cantonese, pepper steak, asparagus hollandaise, and big greasy cheeseburgers. Within arm's reach is a decanter of Wolfschmidt peppermint schnapps. Centered at your table is a gigantic cake in the form of a carrier, and tiny aircraft launch and land by signal from an unseen control booth.

"Alongside the cake are gifts from all your friends—a new

K-model Harley-Davidson Tourister with a Bates seat, an altimeter for your Cessna 182, and a hundred-pound set of Wilson rubber-coated weights. Someone hands you an envelope, and you read its contents: Tonight you will drive home in your new Mercedes-Benz!

"While you are acknowledging your gifts with thanks, you are interrupted by fireworks and flashing strobe lights. Out of the cake pops Susie, dressed in a scanty bright orange bikini. She runs down the top of the table and presses her lithe body against you. She kisses you hard on the lips, and once again the crowd stands to applaud."

For forty-five minutes I gave Palmer the best birthday party I could dream up. He was still in trouble with the V for the crazy caper a year earlier and was doing time in solitary. Palmer had also broken his arm and was sure the V had set it wrong and that it would never heal. He was depressed, and I hoped that the nasal communication through a cup opposite his wall would cheer him up.

I knew everything there was to know about Palmer—his favorite food and drink, the things he always wanted to own, and the girl in Los Angeles he had wanted to marry but never had the courage to ask. Palmer laughed at the fantasy and cried with nostalgia.

* * *

POWs celebrated anything and everything—birthdays, anniversaries, religious holidays, Groundhog Day, Jewish Independence Day. We were always looking for excuses to bolster morale.

Ed Hubbard and I once called up Ev Alvarez at the morning gong. We knew he would put his ear to a specific spot for maximum volume, and Ed and I placed our cups about two feet on either side. I said, "Good morning, Everett. This is Room 4, bringing you"—and Ed continued "a happy birthday in living stereo." Then he heard us sing "Happy Birthday" from two speakers. (We didn't have to worry about balance . . . Ev could listen with only one ear at a time.)

Mike Christian once told me that his one dream in life was to win something. Several months later as his birthday neared, I decided to make his dream come true. I got up each night and quietly started forming the pieces of wire I'd collected. I then put toilet paper and rice glue around the form, scraped whitewash off the wall, and applied it to the paper. During the day I hid it under my rack, and finally one night I completed the project. On his birthday I watched my mate's eyes light up with surprise and laughter. He was holding his trophy, a loving cup with the inscription "The Best Bull Shooter in the Whole World."

The last New Year's Day I decided that we should play a trick on Lew, and talked three or four guys into helping me write a skit. Lew Shattuck was one of the POWs who had lost an eye and wore a homemade green eye patch. He had another problem which he had shared with several other men. He had been engaged before he became a POW, but as years passed, he began to have second thoughts about Dianne. All the while, she wrote letters and sent pictures of herself sitting on his father's lap or playing homemaker with his mother. This circumstance was perfect for a situation comedy.

The setting: Repatriation Day. Lew, played by Don Waltman, is coming home. He steps off the airplane and there is Dianne in all her splendor. (Dianne is performed by Bill Metzger who wears three straw brooms for hair and wadded clothing to create an enormous bustline.) Lew says, "How wonderful it is to be back! Dianne, we must talk about something." But Dianne is so excited and amorous that she doesn't listen.

The second act is in the lobby of a hotel. Lew is trying to sign the register while Dianne drags him away from the desk. She is shouting, "Oh, this is going to be wonderful! I have a surprise I want to show you!" She continues to hint about her surprise and refuses to let Lew confess his change of heart.

The third act is in the bedroom. After a few more puns and one-liners, Dianne announces, "It's time to show you the surprise—here is your seven-year-old son! Eddie, meet your daddy." Ed Hubbard prances out on the makeshift stage wearing a diaper and carrying a cardboard lollypop. Lew looks down and says, "That's not *my* kid!" Dianne answers, "Of course he is. He's got your eyes!" With that, little Eddie turns to the audience and hanging from his brow is a homemade green eye patch.

* * *

Christmas 1968 was bleak. The V had lied about the packages we were supposed to receive. As a poor substitute, I gave my cellmates a tiny Santa Claus which I had carved from a little piece of lye soap.

Christmas 1969 was a little better. My cellmates and I made a three-foot Christmas tree from mosquito netting shaped like a funnel. We had saved tinfoil from packages and at that time had a deck of black and red cards which we spread on the rack for decoration.

The three succeeding Christmases, isolation was for the most part behind us. In 1970 we were in the big rooms at the Hilton and we really wanted to celebrate. I felt the urge to plan a gala holiday with the biggest Christmas tree in Viet Nam, so I designed one to go all the way to the ceiling in one of the corners. On the top was to be a two-foot tinfoil star. Toilet paper and rags would form sweeping branches. Paper and tinfoil ornaments would be cut into shapes of balls and

diamonds. Toilet paper popcorn strings would be colored with cherry and lime Kool-Aid we'd received in packages. At the base of the tree would be the inscription PEACE ON EARTH made from torn pieces of multicolored tinfoil, creating a mosaic effect. Above one wall would be eighteen-inch letters spelling MERRY CHRISTMAS. On the opposite wall would be a five-foot holly wreath with a big red bow.

We knew the V would not allow this. They had told us many times that if we wanted to have Christmas, they would give us anything we needed. Experience told us however that when we accepted anything from them, we also accepted the propaganda that went along with it. None of us were willing to erect a tree with all the trimmings while photographers took pictures showing the great joy of captivity.

A month before Christmas we started making and hiding the ornaments. Toilet paper was rationed for popcorn strings. We were preparing a program, which included the Christmas story and carols. Quincy Collins would direct the choir.

Late at night on 23 December we stood on bed pallets to trim the tree and spell out the greeting. It was a tough job but a joyous one. We continued into the morning of the twenty-fourth, and still the work was not complete. Within an hour we could finish hanging the few remaining ornaments and sticking the last few letters of CHRISTMAS to the wall.

When out on the lawn there arose such a clatter. It wasn't St. Nicholas that was the matter. It was the camp commander.

Here they came! The V stormed in and took all of us out into the courtyard. While we waited, guards returned to rip and tear everything they could reach. Instead of throwing the ornaments out, they wadded them up and strewed them on the floor. They took everything else we had—pictures, letters, package items, clothes—and piled our belongings into blankets, threw the bundles over their backs, and carried them away.

Two hours later the room was bare except for decorations they couldn't reach. We were told to strip naked for a search. Guards looked in our mouths and rectums for hidden articles. Except for the shorts and shirts we wore, we had nothing. Christmas Eve . . . and our toys were gone.

As soon as I was taken back to the cell and the guards had left, I immediately went to the mangled tree. Unwadding pieces of paper, I was able to repair most of the tree and PEACE ON EARTH, but MERRY CHRISTMAS was too far gone. All of the package items that we'd been saving—coffee, chocolate, candy—were also gone. Nevertheless, we would not soon forget the pleasures of working together on a project that brought us closer to home.

In 1971 I spent Christmas with three men in the Zoo. One of the men, A4 Pilot Danny Glenn, had been on the *Kitty Hawk* and was the first man to be shot down on my cruise. Danny had studied architecture and had a lot of artistic talent.

Early in November I asked him, "What are we going to do for Christmas? Maybe we could have a program—sing, say a few Bible verses, and offer a prayer. It would be great if we could have a nativity scene right there on that wall. Do you think you could come up with one?"

"Yeah, I think so. I'll give it a try."

I had no idea of the possibilities, but with his talent he created a masterpiece that could have been shown in the Louvre or El Prado.

Of course, Danny had no paint, no brush, no canvas. Everything was improvised. He carried in bricks from outside and sampled them by color—from off-white to purple. He then ground the bricks into dust, and by adding ash or scrapings of paint, he found he could manufacture nearly any color in the spectrum. For blue, he scraped off residue from a toothpaste tube. Grinding bricks hour after hour for several weeks, he collected enough dust for his project.

Then Danny pulled out some of his hair and tied it to a bamboo stick to make a brush. With ashes, he roughed out three church windows on the wall about five feet in height, and we concealed the outline with hanging clothes.

About four days before Christmas, he started adding the color. Shadows were made from various shades of ashes. Rays of starlight broke up the grays with white and yellow. In the center window was Joseph and the Virgin Mary and Baby Jesus in a manger. On the right panel were the shepherds, and on the left, the Magi. The details were exquisite. Mary's smile paralleled da Vinci's *La Gioconda*. I was really impressed. Even if the work had not been done in prison, this triptych was worthy of the finest galleries.

While Dan worked on the wall, I started to write on toilet paper a four-part arrangement of carols so that we could sing in harmony. We also made gifts for other rooms—bread-dough rosaries and cigarette cases of homemade cardboard. We put the cases in toilet paper wrapping and toilet paper ribbons and toilet paper bows. Just a few more hours were needed to complete the shepherds.

We passed the day of the twenty-fourth without incident. Toward sunset, however, a guard peeked through the flap and saw a marred wall. We could hear him yell all the way back to the "head shed." Inevitably, an officer rushed to the room. "That are not allowed. You destroy now or you severely punish!"

I asked, "Can we save it one more day? Tomorrow is Christmas!"

"No. Wash off now!"

It was a sad thing to do, but with buckets of water we washed away a masterpiece. Afterwards, we were taken out of the cell and again everything we owned was riddled. The V took the gifts for the other prisoners, and package items, and all my music.

We arose the next day and sang the carols as best we could and pretended to see the Baby Jesus lying in an imaginary manger. We said our prayers and had our simple Christmas.

At each Christmas the V gave us a special meal, and in all fairness I must say that it was not bad. We were given turkey or some beef, an egg-roll, and sometimes a little glass of wine or a half cup of beer. We even had green onions. Everyone was sick the next day but we didn't care: we were happy to taste something with seasoning.

The V had discovered our Christmas projects and were angry for what we'd done. The next day, however, they came in all smiles and said, "Even if you criminals break camp regulations, we gracious camp authority give another chance and want show goodwill by give special dinner."

The first few years they did this, photographers were behind them. Often we refused to go outside our rooms to pick up the food. We figured that if they wanted to take pictures, they could snap us eating pumpkin soup. The last three years we ate Christmas dinners without charge except for a "Christmas meal was good" statement in our letters home.

Another year passed, and it was Christmas 1972. For two years in a row we had been wiped out, so this year was going to be bigger and better than ever.

We had been moved to Dogpatch, a mountain camp with no electricity. I was in a building which had been designed to house two men to a room. The cells were too crowded to take a step, but the V did allow us into the hallway for six or seven hours of the day, and during that time we could visit prisoners from seven other cells.

Nevertheless, Dogpatch was dreary. The sun went behind the mountains at about four o'clock and with no electricity, we spent fourteen hours in darkness each day. The V gave us lamps, but never enough kerosene.

With our rooms so dark, I came up with the idea of a slide show. As luck would have it, I was with Danny Glenn again, and I knew his talent.

"Danny, what should we do this Christmas?"

Danny was a slow talker, a kind of Will Rogers Oklahoman. "Well, Charlie, the last one was a total disaster. I don't know what we're gonna do."

"How about a slide show?"

"Well, I don't know . . . maybe so."

One night Danny and I shifted roommates so that we were locked up in the same cell. We got out a little homemade lamp and started experimenting with slits and holes in pieces of paper. We needed to know how far away we could get from the wall and still have definition. The clearest picture required a gigantic slide (the smaller the slide, the fuzzier the details). We compromised with pieces about eight inches high and twelve inches across.

We needed a projector. Fortunately we found a piece of tarpaper and bent it into a tube four inches in diameter and fourteen inches in height. Danny did most of the work on this project, spending hours in experimentation. We cut a square in the tarpaper and attached a flap so that the hole could be opened and closed by pulling on a string. With a flame glowing inside the tube, the light could be directed toward the slide held a few inches from the hole.

The paper slides represented scenes corresponding to

carols. The first song would be "O Little Town of Bethlehem," and Danny would raise the flap to show a cutout
skyline of Bethlehem. While prisoners would sing, "Yet in
thy dark street shineth the everlasting light," Danny would
raise the flap further to reveal the guiding star.

We practiced several weeks. It was difficult because we
could cut out a silhouette and still not know what would
show up on the wall. We decided to have Christmas on the
twenty-third this time. On the twenty-second, however, in
came Rat—the officer clearly capable of sadism. He picked up
our slides and asked, "What this? You know if break
regulation you be severely punish!"

Both Dan and I pleaded with Rat, asking for lenient,
humane treatment and for just one night to be left alone. We
tried to show him how the slides worked, but daylight didn't
permit it. I got the impression that Rat thought it was a piece
of junk. Since he knew that the war was all but over, that his
capital city was being bombed, and that our projector and
slides were harmless, he consented to our pleas.

We decided to move the program to Christmas Eve, and
this time it went without a flaw. As a matter of fact, we had
two showings and each audience was packed—Christians,
Jews, atheists, everyone except the V.

In total darkness I announced that I would recite Bible
verses describing the birth of our Savior, Jesus Christ, and as I
began each song the prisoners should join in. Then I started
singing "O Little Town of Bethlehem. . . ." Danny opened
the flap slowly and, like a curtain rising, exposed the skyline.
The panorama broadened to include the stars and shepherds
in the fields. About an hour later the program was over, and
prisoners returned to their cells quiet and happy.

homecoming

"When are we going home?"

This question circulated among POWs more than any other. With varying degrees of pessimism and optimism, we sought clues for the elusive answer. Since we figured the V would try to fatten us up a little before we came home, an especially lumpy bowl of soup meant time to "pack suitcases." Some prisoners relied heavily on that idea, and became tagged as "gastronomers."

Gastronomers soon learned how imperfect their science was. In March 1972, when the V army failed in an all-out thrust at the DMZ, we thought they would be forced to sue for peace. Our food had improved, and the gastronomers looked once more into unusually mushy bowls for clair-voyance. The subject of their prophecies was too serious for us to laugh away, especially when their predictions didn't come true.

Two hundred and six of us were high in the mountains

near the Chinese border at Camp Dogpatch when a very interesting thing happened. On 25 October, V officers came into our cells and said, "Bliss, Browning—out. . . . Sandvick, Sullivan—out. . . ." These men rolled up their clothing and left for another section of the camp. The rest of us paced the floor and wondered what it all meant. No, they weren't being pulled out by alphabetical order, nor by the number of letters they had received. They were being arranged by order of shoot-down.

One of our plums stipulated that the order of release was the sick and injured, the enlisted men, the officers by shoot-down. It appeared that the V themselves were making preparations to abide by that plum. Our optimism flourished.

One morning that November the V called everyone in my building out into the courtyard and read a portion of the secret talks at Paris. It was a peace treaty! We reached higher and higher emotional peaks as the interpreter delineated the cease-fire and repatriation procedures. Just as he was down to signatures, he looked up and said, "However . . . stubborn U.S. officials refuse sign honorable treaty." He read on, and for fifteen minutes he told us how bellicose and obdurate our representatives were for not signing. Naturally, the news was disappointing, but it was good to know that wheels were turning.

We were still in Dogpatch when bombs started dropping over Hanoi on 12 December. Some prisoners thought this was sound strategy, that it would hasten our return home. I must admit, however, that I was afraid. When I found out about it, I went back to my cell and started squaring away for six more years of captivity. I was afraid that the B52 raids would only tighten North Vietnamese unity and prolong the war.

Although the bombing was intense, and although American prisoners in Hanoi were close to the targets, I suppose that Kay Russell and I still held the record for taking the nearest miss. During a fierce raid in June 1967—only one month after I was shot down—Kay and I were under our bunks and being bounced off the concrete floor by bomb and artillery explosions. Suddenly, the dungeon gray of our cell became an intense white, and I was momentarily blinded. Rocks showered to the floor—then clanking of rebounding metal.

I yelled over to Kay, "What was that?"

"I think it's a shell!"

When the roar of the planes diminished, we crawled out to see a hole the size of a grapefruit in our wall. Lying at our feet was a smoldering 20 mm armor-piercing tracer. When we saw we were both OK, our fear turned to laughter. What we once called a strike was now a raid, worthy of daily discussion.

January 1973 . . . and another new year. We somehow felt this might be our last. During siesta on 19 January, we peeked out cracks and saw a large congregation of armed V soldiers dressed in new uniforms gathering in the courtyard. On the command, they formed a sloppy rank and file. Flags and banners waved as soldiers received medals and praise. Then they broke rank and ran all directions to start stacking supplies.

Nightfall, and still the guards scurried with lock boxes. Then we heard a roar, and the front gate opened wide to allow truck after truck into the camp. We'd never seen so many vehicles—eighteen or twenty of them!

About two o'clock the next morning, officers came to our cells and gave the order: "Roll up. Leave camp." We didn't know where we were going, and of course the V wouldn't tell us. We put on every stitch of clothing we owned to protect us from the January cold and started throwing our blankets onto the trucks. After our gear was loaded, we climbed aboard.

The trucks were one-and-a-half-ton rattletraps with a Conestoga-type bed. Guards directed a dozen or so of us to crowd into the back. V supervisors yelled, "More! More!" and five or six prisoners pushed into little spaces. "More! More!" insisted the officers. Not until the twenty-third prisoner had been pried into the truck were the V satisfied. Guards, stepping over our bodies, handcuffed us in pairs. One guard squeezed to the front, and another, carrying two puppies for chow, squeezed into the back. There we were, cramped like college kids in a phone booth—twenty-five of us . . . and two squealing puppies.

The sky was still pitch black as we started down the rough mountain road. I noticed that between the cab and the bed of the truck was a fifty-five-gallon barrel. Because it had no bung, gasoline started sloshing and spilling over us and our gear. The fumes were so strong and we were so hot that several prisoners started vomiting. We needed air, but the guards refused to open the flaps.

So that they could see, the V hung a kerosene lantern from the overhead metal support. As it dangled back and forth, I envisioned twenty-three charred Americans handcuffed together by pairs. We were helpless. There was no way out. Several of the men started *bao-cao*ing to draw attention to the lantern. After minutes of explanation, the men finally conveyed the danger to the rear guard. Just as he put out the lamp, the guard in front pulled out a cigarette and a match. We hollered, but not soon enough to keep him from striking it. Fortunately, only the cigarette went up in smoke.

Our latrine was the same rusted bucket that we had been using for years. Because we were handcuffed and immobile, it was nearly impossible to relieve ourselves. Only the hope of repatriation made the situation bearable.

I remembered back to the time a fireman had shown me how to get a stuck ring off a finger. He had wrapped string tightly in front of the ring, and the ring slipped off easily. Could this method be applied to a manacle? I had stashed away some string and decided to give it a try. I was surprised how small I could make my hand by wrapping it. I forced the manacle, scraping off skin, and at last I was free—and so was my partner Joe Crecca. Obviously, both of us would have to remain very close together. Guards would otherwise notice and accuse us of trying to escape. At least we would be free to act in an emergency.

It was a terrible trip, lasting till nightfall the following day. The road was snaked with hairpin curves and pocked with deep holes. Instead of applying brakes, the driver pushed in the clutch and let the truck gain speed at each downward slope. I'm certain that we were going at least sixty miles per hour. Puppies were flung from front to back. It was the most exciting roller-coaster ride I've ever had!

I kept working my hand in and out of the manacle until I no longer needed the string. I passed it down to the next pair, and before long most prisoners were independent of their partners. If we were to go over a cliff, we might have a little better chance of survival. The guards never knew what we had done; in fact, they were so naïve that they handed prisoners their rifles and grenades while they crawled around the truck. We could have taken control of the truck very easily, but we wouldn't have known what to do with it once we had it. Had we felt that settlement of the war was nowhere in sight, I'm sure we would have tried something.

I had also concealed a razor blade and cut a hole in the tarp so that I could see out. Still unsure of our destination, I was happy to see familiar rickety pontoons over the Red River. That meant we were heading back to Hanoi; and because we had traveled during daylight hours we assumed the bombing had ceased. And if it had, the war was probably coming to an end.

We entered the capital city, and for the fifth time I waited at the front gate of the Hilton while doors to the tunnel clanked open. It was like old home week; I knew right where to go. I was led to the same room where I had designed North Viet Nam's largest Christmas tree two years before. The little hooks to drape toilet paper were still there and so was my name—scratched into the wall. Only my cellmates were different.

During the week of 21-28 January 1973, for the first time, treatment was actually humane. The V set up a volleyball net and allowed us to play or to exercise. They gave us books and magazines from home. We *knew* something was happening!

About 8:00 a.m. on the twenty-ninth, the V camp commander stormed in with a complaint. He told us that we were not making full use of the freedom we had been given. Instead of suddenly turning our faces and walking back to our cells, we were supposed to stay out in the courtyard and enjoy the sun and the exercise. When he finished, he asked through his interpreter, "You any questions?" Our senior officer Ev Southwick asked, "What has transpired at Paris?"

"Nothing happen Paris. No talk going on. War last long time. You live peaceful and play volleyball."

An hour later, the camp commander once again called our group together—about 180 of us old-timers. It was the first time that all prisoners in the camp were gathered in one place. (The newer prisoners were staying at the Plantation.) We lined up by buildings in military formation and were called to attention by our acting wing commander, Lieutenant Colonel Norm Gaddis. Although V officials did not recognize our rank structure, they said nothing. The camp commander read an announcement, and the interpreter read the translation. It had been a long time since I'd heard English worded so professionally.

When he finished and told us that we could go, our wing commander again called us to attention and dismissed us. With heads bowed, we walked quietly back to our rooms. We were stunned. Some had waited for these words for over eight and one-half years. The war was over. We were going home.

* * *

Two days later each of us was given a copy of the peace settlement. The agreement stipulated that we would all be released within sixty days. The first to go would be the sick and injured. Following them would be the enlisted men and the officers in order of shoot-down, just as had been designed in the plum.

For once the Vietnamese had thought ahead. As soon as we entered the Hilton, we were divided into groups so that about ninety officers were quartered on one side of the camp and the remaining ninety on the other. New clothes and shoes and little overnight cases were stacked in bundles. We were taken out to stand on pieces of toilet paper while guards penciled lines around both feet. We were finally going to wear real shoes!

On the morning of 12 February we peeked to the other side of the camp to see twenty-four American prisoners of war form a platoon. Their SRO gave the "Fo'ard harch," and tears welled in my eyes as I watched POW No. 1 Ev Alvarez, dressed in blue trousers, gray jacket, and black shoes, march out of the prison gate. His hell was finally over. I saw an

American aircraft fly overhead—this time with no bombs. It was like a dream!

On the thirteenth the V officers rearranged cellmates. Twenty of us were taken out of our cells and led to the New Guy Village, the area of my initial imprisonment. I couldn't believe what I saw. The chipped green knobs were still there, and blood was still on the walls. But everything was so much smaller! The tree, instead of growing, had shrunk. Six years earlier, I would have described it as being three feet in diameter, but now it seemed a third that size. The doorframes, the tile, the height, width, breadth of the rooms and buildings were miniatures of what I'd remembered. Six years earlier I had concentrated on every detail, but I must have been in such a state of shock that everything seemed expanded. I looked around the New Guy Village with disgust. If the V were trying to appease us with improved treatment, taking us back to torture rooms was no way to do it.

We saw no reason why we had been separated from our fellow prisoners, but late that night the camp commander informed us what was to happen. He explained that Dr. Henry Kissinger was visiting Hanoi and that he had twenty empty seats on his airplane that he wanted filled. We were told to gather our belongings and to be ready to leave within the hour.

Something was very wrong. Even though we were in the 115-man ready release group and would be next to go, we weren't the first twenty of that group. As a matter of fact, I was about ninety-fifth on the waiting list. Our SRO Jim Pirie explained to the camp commander that we would follow the procedure as stated in the Paris agreement. To that, the V official answered, "You make mistake. We come later. Maybe you change mind. No trick. Other prisoners leave few days after you."

In the same hour the camp commander returned, carrying what appeared to be an official document printed by computer. "Here proof. Kissinger come for you. You not abide by orders, you cause international incident. Plane leave tomorrow morning."

He handed Jim the document, an IBM sheet which contained our names, ranks, serial numbers, dates of capture, etc. The V had never used such a printout. Indeed, they were lucky to have a typewriter. Jim looked at the camp commander and answered, "We cannot accept this as proof. We do not know that Dr. Kissinger has been here. You may be trying to deceive us."

"Tomorrow morning plane come. You take bath, shave, put on new clothes for go home."

"We will do those things," Jim responded, "but we'll wait until tomorrow before we make a decision."

The twenty of us, cleaning up and trying on our new clothes, were exhilarated even if we didn't know where or when we were going. All of us were united in one thought, however: we would not double-cross our fellow prisoners. We would not leave out of order.

The next morning Jim made the decision. "Men, put your clothes back into the box and leave 'em there. If the V insist we go, they'll have to handcuff us and use ropes to drag us out." Jim hoped he was making the right decision. Lieutenant Colonel Norm Gaddis was our senior officer in the camp, but we had no communication with him.

"Why not establish comm with Norm?" I asked. "If they serve chow this morning, they will bring a pot over here. The guys who are washing pots are on his side of the camp. Let's put a note on the bottom of the pot so that the dishwashers can relay our problem to Norm."

"Good idea, Charlie," Jim agreed. "Write one out."

I prepared the note, stating that the V had come up with an official-looking document with orders for us to leave. I also asked what would happen if we didn't comply with what might be Kissinger's wishes. I stuck the note on the bottom of the pot and watched the guards tote it away.

That afternoon we were served potatoes; and when Jim cut into his, he found a note from Colonel Gaddis: "Don't go. Demand see me or U.S. rep." Jim had picked the right potato.

By that time the Vietnamese were getting restless. Ranking generals and high state department officials rushed to New Guy Village to convince us that everything was legitimate and that we should leave. Jim countered their appeals with the demand to see an American representative. Of course, the V refused to let any American official inside the prison to see our miserable quarters. Jim responded, "OK, we're not going!"

"OK," the V official replied, "you not go!"

On 17 February we moved back into the original cell and rejoined our mates. We were happy that we had not betrayed our buddies. Still, we were confused: Why did they select us? In our group were some real tough nuts who had given the V a lot of trouble. Others had tried to get along with their guards and officers.

Later that afternoon Bob Wideman was taken out of our cell and Jim Bailey was moved in. Jim, scheduled to go in a later group, had been transported to the Hilton from the Plantation. The V had informed him that he would leave with our group because his father was seriously ill. That information was our first clue that perhaps all of us had problems at home.

On the evening of the seventeenth the V complied with Pirie's demands and took him away to meet with our senior officer, Norm Gaddis. They then told Norm, "Order Jim tell men go home!" Norm retorted with an emphatic *no*. Norm was led back to his cell, and once again the V entreated, "You go now?"

"No!" Jim responded. "I must first see an American representative. If he tells me to go, I'll follow his orders."

They took Jim from our side and into a nice section of the camp. There he met with American free men—an Air Force lieutenant colonel and a major—one a pilot of the C130 transport and the other a member of the U.S. delegation.

Jim walked up to the man and saluted. The salute was returned, and one of the men said angrily, "What the hell are you guys doing?"

"They're trying to kick us out of here *out of order.*"

"What do you mean—out of order? We've been busting our gut for eight years trying to get you guys home. We're gonna take you any way we can!"

"Wait just a minute. We have our rules, too. We've read the agreement and it says that we leave in order of shoot-down. These guys the V have selected are *not* the next twenty men. Now do you want to take us out of order? It's your decision."

"OK . . . we'll take you."

Jim was again granted his demand to see Colonel Gaddis. Shortly thereafter he came back to our cell and announced, "OK . . . the colonel has permitted us to leave early." Nineteen prisoners were unanimous in thoughts and words: "That's not enough, Jim. We're not going with permission. We're not leaving at all unless we are *ordered* to go!"

Jim requested to see Colonel Gaddis once more. By now the Vietnamese were going wild. They couldn't understand what was happening, but they thought there was hope. They gave Jim free rein to run back and forth and probably appreciated the fact that their military wasn't the only one bound by red tape.

Colonel Gaddis followed Jim back to our cell. In a tremendous speech, Norm explained how we had been caught in an unfortunate circumstance and that there would be no stigma attached to our untimely departure. He assured us that if any prisoner uttered a word of condemnation, he would be the first to defend our action. At that point, he ordered us to leave camp.

We went back to New Guy Village, put on our clothes and shoes, lined up two by two, and marched out of tunnel gates and into sunlight.

* * *

Ho Chi Minh had promised years earlier that at the end of the war American prisoners would leave with changed hearts and would extol the virtues of North Viet Nam. He said that his country would festoon us with flowers and that the streets would be lined with dancing girls. We saw neither flowers nor dancing girls, but we did see smiling, waving children lined up with their schoolmasters along the streets. A police escort preceded us, and an extra bus followed ours just to make sure no more incidents would occur at the last minute. Leaving Hanoi, we were driven atop a dike that protected the city from the Red River. From this elevation we saw bomb craters and attempts at reconstruction all along the route. And then above us circled the beautiful C141. It dropped landing gear and made the approach to Gia Lam.

Before we entered the airport's gates the bus stopped at a little station to allow use of restrooms. We were offered beer, but I refused. I wanted to be in full control. I wanted to enjoy this part.

At the airport the bus halted near pockmarked runways.

We exited solemnly through a crowd of people and by microphone were told to walk to our receiving officer when our names were called. As I heard my name, I stepped past a table where Vietnamese and American representatives marked off the exchange. I saluted a colonel, then another, and was escorted by an officer who was so excited he could say nothing more than, "Isn't it great! It's so nice to have you back! We've all been waiting for you! Isn't it great!" I felt as though he had previously composed what he would say, but in his excitement his record stuck. Nevertheless, he was right. It *was* great.

I walked up the ramp of the C141 and saw the first Navy uniform. The officer inside that uniform grabbed me and hugged me and told me his name. I didn't know him until he told me he was the briefing officer on the *Kitty Hawk* the day I was shot down. Gary Morrow and I had once worked many hours together and now we could joyfully recall old times.

As soon as I was in the airplane, a nurse kissed me and started the first of a long chain of flashbulbs. We were given American cigarettes, magazines, and information sheets telling us what to expect at Clark Air Force Base.

The pilot taxied down the runway, pushed the throttles, and at the moment of liftoff, suddenly it hit us. We were off North Vietnamese soil! We screamed above the noise of the jets. Minutes later we were soaring above the Gulf of Tonkin and saw some of our ships. The commander of the Seventh Fleet sent a message of welcome and Jim returned the radio comm with a thankful acknowledgment. Someone gave me a dollar bill, and I asked everyone to sign it. Another person handed me a *Playboy,* and I was astonished at its change.

By nightfall we reached the Philippines and Clark AFB. As soon as the doors opened, we could see and hear the enthusiasm from what must have been five thousand people. Banners and bands, choral groups and cheerleaders—everyone seemed to be there.

I walked down the ramp, saluted a general and then an admiral. As I shook the admiral's hand, I was so overcome with emotion that I hugged him. He returned the embrace. Pictures were snapped, and this "make-out" wirephoto was distributed for nationwide coverage.

Military police established lines to keep the crowds from our buses, but they failed: lines were crossed and people reached up to windows to give us flags, flowers, and welcome-home buttons. As we entered the hospital rooms for medical debriefings, we saw on every floor a wallpaper of letters and posters from school children. Many were personalized to Lieutenant Commander Joseph Charles Plumb, and I was deeply touched by the concern of so many people I'd never known.

After a quick physical examination, I dressed in new clothing and attended a briefing from the base commander. It was time for dinner, and as we entered the cafeteria, we marveled at the cuisine. Food ranged from hash to lobster and drink from buttermilk to champagne. I think the chefs were a little disappointed when I asked for ham and eggs and chocolate ice cream.

Tailors worked all night to alter uniforms. The next morning I asked to go to several schools to give my thanks to the students. It was wonderful to see the innocence and enthusiasm of children after so long a time. Their curiosity and uninhibited laughter reflected the essence of freedom.

We boarded another C141, flew to Hawaii for refueling, and at the same time enjoyed a reception by the commander of the Seventh Fleet. Four hours later we circled the Golden

Gate Bridge and landed in San Francisco. Another reception awaited us there.

At each point—Clark, Hawaii, San Francisco—I received VIVA bracelets. The people who wore them were particularly emotional and sometimes almost possessive—as though I belonged to them. After all, they had proudly displayed my name until the nickel-plating had begun to wear away, and they had said many prayers for my safe return. I was the mystery they had included in their private lives, and now that I was real they wanted to touch me and hold me and compare me to their preconceptions.

At Chicago I exited a C9 as its only passenger. In freezing wind and snow hundreds of people hushed as I stepped to the mike and delivered a public acknowledgment of thanks. I was then taken to the hospital where there were more cheering people and waiting doctors. At last I was asked, "Would you like to see your parents?"

"Yes. Certainly."

I found out much later that records were being kept of my every action: "Mr. and Mrs. J. C. Plumb joined their son in a very happy reunion. Commander Plumb kissed and hugged his mother, shook hands with and embraced his father. After a short period of the usual greetings, Commander Plumb and his parents went into his room and poured soft drinks. Commander Plumb appeared weary but very enthusiastic and pleased to visit. . . ." And so the record continued for the next two weeks. Two days after my arrival, my sister Carol and my brothers Larry and Brad flew up to Chicago, and for the first time in eleven years all of our family were together.

Also during that period I started intelligence debriefings to identify every name and face I could recall from my years in prison. I paged through book after book filled with pictures of men who had been shot down and were still missing. Intelligence officers had spent many hours and did an excellent job in their thorough search for clues revealing the fate of missing soldiers. I was sorry to tell them that, as far as I knew, their list of verified POWs was complete and that it was unlikely American soldiers were being withheld by the Vietnamese.

* * *

On 4 March I left Chicago for home. On Kansas City's largest private jet, I reached home base in rain and fog. More than eight hundred people with signs and posters were huddled inside an empty hanger. Roger Pilley, my best buddy at Shawnee Mission North, had arranged a grand and glorious homecoming. I went to the podium and expressed my gratefulness for the concerns and prayers of so many people. Dignitaries from both Kansas and Missouri were present, and the mayors of cities in the metropolitan area presented keys. The hangar resounded with "Hello, Charlie" to the tune of "Hello, Dolly."

After a press conference, I was taken home in a limousine with police escort. When I got there, relatives and friends were watching me on television. It was especially fun to greet uncles and aunts and cousins, the younger ones for the first time.

Gifts started pouring in. I was given the use of a new Ford. I received vacations to Florida and New York. I spoke at many schools and organizations, telling them of my experiences and especially of my appreciation for their concern. As a kind of sabbatical from a hectic pace, I asked my brother Brad to go with me to the Caribbean to do a little scuba diving.

One of the most pleasant evenings I had, however, was planned by my former drama coach, Virnelle Fletcher. She had corresponded with many of my fellow thespians and once again directed them in scenes from high school plays in which I had acted. As I watched them perform my part, I found myself mouthing familiar lines.

Late on the evening of my return, my parents and Brad, Roger and his date, the Fletchers, and I relaxed in a quiet country club. My mouth watered as a Kansas City steak was set before me, and I was reminded of the gastronomers. Their final prediction had been wrong! My last meal at the Hilton had been a bowl of thin cabbage soup . . . but I had gulped it down as though it were good.

divorce

The band had played a spirited "Anchors Away" as I stepped from the dock and walked up the officer's prow to the *Kitty Hawk*. It was the first time I had left Anne since our marriage, and when I reached the top, I turned to the rail and once more waved good-bye. Anne had been dependent on me, and I had allowed her to be. Now she stood alone in the stretching shadows of the floating giant. She tried to hold back her tears, but she could not.

I was melancholy, too. Anne and I had been happy together and considered ourselves very fortunate to have such a successful marriage. Both of us had similar backgrounds and interests, and never once had we raised our voices in anger. We had tried to celebrate, but this time Anne's birthday was not a happy one.

While I was on cruise, we lightened somewhat the burden of separation by faithful communication. Anne wrote letters every day and sent tapes twice each week. I carried my tape recorder with me to various parts of the ship to record messages at every opportunity. Occasionally I called her by radio transmission.

After I was shot down, I was of course frustrated and disoriented, but my greatest concern was for Anne. I remembered the Christmas during our courtship and pictured an anxious girl who had suffered from a nervous disorder characterized by terrible hives and edema. I knew that, even if she would have no physical pain, she would certainly have mental anguish. Throughout each day I prayed that she would have peace of mind, that she would be able to endure. In one of my first letters as a POW I told her that I was praying just before bedtime and asked her to pray along with me. Our closest moments had always been those times we had prayed together, and now our only recourse was to unite in prayer in time if not in place.

It seemed that every plan I made in prison centered around Anne, and it was not uncommon for me to outline minute by minute the activities we would share. Weekdays, weekends, holidays, and seasons of the year were carefully scheduled in my dreams. I planned vacations, house parties, evenings at concerts, birthday celebrations for the children we would have. After I came back, not a moment would be wasted. (I'm sure that I hadn't planned enough time for us to kick off shoes and simply relax.) My foremost thought was to be the perfect husband to Anne and father to our future children.

But in the back of my mind lurked the possibility that my prayers for her peace of mind would be answered with the second alternative: she would find happiness without me. I didn't allow myself to dwell on this thought, although it caught me off guard probably once a week. I told myself that a broken relationship was out of the question, and yet, influenced I suppose by my military training, I was destined to consider all of the possibilities. That included the idea of coming home a single man. It wasn't easy to picture myself in that role. I had little desire to do anything without her at my side.

I knew Anne would be changed. I didn't know what her attitudes would be, and I must have spent hundreds of hours choosing the words I would use during that first phone call. Should I be enthusiastic? Or sad? Would I cry? Or would I try to make light of our terrible separation? How would I know? When I left, Anne was "red, white, and blue," but during our isolation she may have become extremely disenchanted with the war. In that case, a victory speech would do nothing to enhance our marriage. I needed to understand exactly how she felt about me, about the war, about the military, and I thought that it would be best to call my father first to find out what she would want to hear.

Mail from Anne during 1972 had become sparse, and I became quite concerned. I had received several letters in 1971 and had anticipated even more the following year. Then, in September, I received a letter which allayed my anxiety. It was a standard letter in which Anne sent her love and said she hoped that I would soon be coming home. One thing puzzled me, however, and that was in the address. In the line which read "Detention Camp for Captured U.S. Pilots," Anne had written *Piolets*. She was an excellent speller, and I wondered why a carefully written letter should contain such an obvious mistake. I would remember to kid her about that when I got home.

* * *

As soon as I boarded the plane at Gia Lam, the first man I talked with was Gary Morrow, an old friend of mine. My first question to him was, "What do you know about Anne?"

Gary said he was sorry, but he had been assigned this flight at the last minute and hadn't had time to find out.

I kept asking everyone the same question. I approached the debriefing medical officers and questioned whether they had brought letters that I could read on the two-hour trip to Clark. They responded in the negative, stating that it was being handled at the hospital and that I could pick up my mail there.

I wasn't the only prisoner who was getting this type of answer. It seemed as though all of our escorts were ill-prepared to receive twenty POWs whose names they'd had for several days. I felt the least they could have done was to bring a few letters along with them.

At the hospital I was issued pajamas and given a room, and several medical officers visited me. My escort entered and opened a complete dossier of pay status and rank promotions. When I asked him about my wife, he dropped his eyes and told me he wasn't sure.

Shortly after he left, a chaplain entered, smiling broadly and delivering elusive questions: "How are you? Isn't it great to be back? After all the excitement and red tape aren't you getting a little tired?"

I looked up at him and said, "Chaplain, I have a great deal of faith in you, and I want you to level with me. So far I haven't been able to get a straight answer from anyone, and I want to know about my wife. Would you please be kind enough to tell me what's going on?"

"Well, Charlie, there *is* a problem with your wife. She is well, but she has had some misgivings. I'm not sure as to the extent, but I am sure that everything is going to be all right. She has written me a letter, but I didn't want to open it. I felt that you should."

"OK. Where's the letter?"

"Well, it's not here right now. It's being brought to my office. We'll have to wait a little while before I can get it."

By then I *was* tired . . . tired of the runaround, but I could see that they wanted to observe me a few more hours before I was hit with a sledgehammer. Finally the chaplain returned and told me he had the letter and that I should come down to his office to read it. I wanted to go, yet I was reluctant. The walk to the office must have paralleled the journey of a condemned man who sensed that his final appeal to the governor had been denied.

Anne's letter was in fact addressed to the chaplain. I opened and read it. She told of her disenchantment and her decision to depart from the present situation. She appealed to the chaplain to break the news as gently as would be possible. The letter said nothing about her having divorced me, or wanting a divorce, or being remarried. Instead, it was quite vague, but clear enough for me to get the message.

I stood up and told the chaplain that I wanted to call my parents; all the while he scrutinized my every action. As I left the office, two chaplains and a sailor were waiting outside the door, backups for whatever might happen. I went to the basement of the hospital and asked the Red Cross ladies if I could call Mom and Dad. They said, "Certainly." I picked up the phone.

Dad answered and greeted me with much enthusiasm. I told him I was sorry that I was a little late getting home, and he answered with a forced laugh. I had determined that I would wait for Dad to break the news to me, so I told him that I was in good health and was anxious to get home and that everything would be fine. Dad could only hem and haw, and so I finally asked, "What about Anne?"

"Oh, she's in good health, but we do have a lot of things to tell you when you get home. Mom and I are going to meet you at the hospital in Chicago—just the two of us—and we can talk about it then. We'll work out something, so don't worry."

I had to get tough. "Come on, Dad. I've been through hell and back, and you're not going to shake me up with anything you can say."

"Yeah, I guess you're right, son. . . . Anne filed for divorce four months ago."

"Well, did she get it?"

"No, the judge denied it . . . wanted to wait until you got home to let you see what you thought about it."

"Has she made definite plans to remarry?"

"No, she hasn't. There may be a chance to work it out, but I think she's pretty set in her ways."

"OK. Let me talk to Mom."

Mom came to the phone and apparently had not heard all of my discussion with Dad. She didn't know that I was already aware of the situation, and she said something which I'll never forget: "Son, I'd give ten years of my life not to have to tell you this."

My eyes got wet and I asked the Red Cross lady for a Kleenex. I could tell right then that the biggest casualty of the divorce was going to be my mother—wrinkles in her brow, gray in her hair, and years already stolen from her.

The telephone conversation ended after about fifteen minutes. In one respect I was relieved to have finally gotten past all the gibberish and to the bottom of the story. It was pretty late, and I went back to my room. I asked for a sleeping pill a couple of hours after I went to bed, but it didn't help. I had to stay awake to face a world of realism.

I was forced to think about bachelorhood. I tried to envision myself living alone in Kansas City or traveling all over the States. The visions wouldn't come. Anne was always somewhere, tagging along behind me, stepping around a corner, waiting at the front porch. Could I be a bachelor in New York? No. How about southern California? No. It was like trying all the bars but being denied entrance because of being underage. I couldn't accept a man who refused to give up his past.

The only place I could remember being happy without Anne was the Philippines. While I was on cruise, I had spent nearly two months there and had so filled my days with exploration that I almost forgot my loneliness. It therefore became very obvious to me that my answer would be to delay my return to the States and to remain in Southeast Asia for an indefinite period of time. I started working out plans to pursue that end, and they came to me rather easily. I felt the Navy could find something for me to do, and for relaxation I could run into Manila and buy a sailboat and generally cool my heels. With these thoughts, I finally dozed off to sleep.

A few hours later, the medical officers came into the room to record my vital signs—heartbeat, temperature, etc. I was still fairly content with the decision I had made during the night. I started asking various people what they thought about my being a professional soldier somewhere in the Orient, and most frequently their response was a wild stare.

That afternoon I asked the escort to take me to several schools to thank the children for their concern. I hadn't seen children for six years, and my spirits soared as I was received with genuine warmth. For two hours I walked from one end of the school to the other, and when I had visited every classroom, the public affairs officer, completely unaware of the divorce situation and my decision to stay in the Orient, said, "Charlie, you really made them sit up and listen. They were honestly interested in what you had to say, and these kids certainly need to hear about your faith in God and your love for the United States. I'm sure you'll help many youngsters when you get home."

I had in fact enjoyed myself, and I felt as though I had communicated with the students. After I thought about it, I decided that I could return home to something—a mission. I would try to guide troubled youngsters. Before the afternoon gave way to dusk, I had made a new decision. If people wanted to listen, I would tell my story.

So I started home. In Hawaii I expected to see the parents of my Naval Academy roommate and best friend, Jim Holian. I didn't see the Holians, but I did see a fellow who was a classmate of mine in high school. I asked, "Did the Holians come?" "No, Charlie, they aren't here." At that point, he showed me a book telling about our class's ten-year reunion. He told where classmates were and what they were doing. Of course, my first question was "What about Anne?"

"She's just dropped out of sight, Charlie. We haven't heard from her at all."

"Well, do you think that's the reason the Holians didn't show up?"

"No, I don't think so. I think that it would have been too painful for them to see you, Charlie. Jim died two years ago from cancer." My stop in Hawaii was the second shock of my pilgrimage.

We then left for San Francisco where a few of the fellows got off. I met the wives of my comrades, and it seemed that I had known these girls as friends for years. In fact, after all the hours of conversation about them, they *had* been friends for years. It was a wonderful reunion.

Then on to St. Louis, where more wives greeted their husbands. I changed planes, and as the C9 taxied out, only two men were on board—Ed Mechenbier and I. We stopped at

Dayton, Ohio, and I stood at the top of the ramp as Ed walked down from the big jet and into the arms of his loving wife.

Then the bird was mine alone. During the flight to Chicago I kept asking myself, "Is there a chance that Anne will be waiting for me?" I forced myself to reject the idea. "No, I've talked to my folks and they say there's no way. It's impossible that she'll be there."

When we taxied down the runway at 2:00 a.m. I caught myself wiping off the windows and scanning the crowd of people, hoping to see a little blonde with tears in her eyes. Anne was not there. My return would be different from the others.

It was at that point that I felt the beginning of the end of my close relationship with Anne. However, it was also the beginning of a special closeness to my parents. Since that time I have been embarrassed to admit that I had ever considered staying in the Philippines: my wonderful, loving parents back in the States had been so concerned about me. I now fully realize how much they sacrificed and how much they suffered on my behalf. My debt to them can never be repaid.

In the hospital room the next day I called Anne. "Yes," she said, "it's true. I'm very sorry. It was a very difficult decision, but one which I had to make. I've filed for divorce. Can we get together when you come home? I'd like to get it all settled as soon as possible."

I talked to several lawyers in Chicago who informed me that Anne had no cause for divorce. She had filed on grounds of desertion, and of course that was not applicable. They advised me that if I wanted to contest, the divorce could be delayed for several months, perhaps years.

Yet Anne had told me that she wanted to remarry. I

would not become an obstacle to her happiness. I called her parents, and they seemed quite unsettled about Anne's decision.

A few days later I called Anne again, and she complained that many members in the news media had been harassing her. She said that she had often been misquoted and was the victim of character assassination.

I then talked personally to some of the newspapermen and told them that I did not want her maligned in any way; in fact, I wanted them to say nothing at all about my wife. For the most part they were receptive to my wishes. I gave them a quote which they could use if they felt they had to: "The divorce is a regrettable but inevitable drifting apart after so many years." By this time, my hope for reconciliation was dead. I was determined to take it on the chin and roll with the punches.

I flew to Kansas City on 4 March and again called Anne to determine a time and place for our meeting. She suggested Tuesday, the sixth, around 1:30 p.m.

"Where shall we meet?" I asked.

"Why don't you come over to my place?"

I had thought about this ahead of time. I just didn't know what our face-to-face reactions would be. I felt that in a private meeting we might become irrational, and the last thing I wanted to do was let a few moments of emotion change the decision she had carefully weighed.

"No, I don't think your place would be a good idea. How about coming over to my folks' home?"

I didn't know it at the time, but she was not on particularly good terms with them. We therefore decided to meet on neutral grounds and chose a popular cafeteria.

At about 1:15, I entered the cafeteria and scoped out the place. I looked for a table that would be semiprivate but still public enough to disallow the emotion of privacy. I saw one by a window and propped the chairs against the table so that no one else would sit there. After I made the selection, I went to the lobby and waited.

From fifty yards away, I saw Anne drive up. When she got out of the car, her hair fell to her shoulders the way it always had, and she walked the same kind of walk that I had always known. Under her arm she carried books and papers.

"Hello, Anne."

"Hello, Charles. How are you?"

I escorted her to the table and soon found her to be congenial. I was immediately engrossed in her personality and was particularly surprised that, instead of wrinkles of time and worry and loneliness, she was as beautiful as the day I had left her.

Both of us tried to be as considerate as we could. Several times she caught herself calling me "Honey," a name she had used throughout our married life. The conversation was proceeding very well under the strained circumstances until she reached down to get tax forms and insurance papers. As her hand came up from underneath the table, I saw on her left hand a big diamond ring.

Of all the things that happened that day, this hurt the most. My wife was wearing an engagement ring which someone else had given her. Her hand no longer wore the modest tiger's eye engagement ring or the wedding band which symbolized our eternal love. I reacted rather sharply. I thought it poor taste to be wearing that ring and asked her not to flash it in front of me. Uneasiness followed.

With the papers were my letters which she had received, and as she pulled them out, she explained her dilemma because of the change in my handwriting. Trying to discover a meaning within my script, she had permitted a graphologist

to study several letters and to write an interpretation of them. Anne told me that she had tried not to take stock in what this handwriting expert had to say, but the thought of my being "rigidly controlled," and "living in a world of [my] own" was a contributing factor in her decision to leave me.

Our final comments were brief.

"Are you bitter toward me?" Anne asked.

"No. I . . . guess I still love you."